AF480679

THE CHANNEL CONUNDRUM

NAVIGATING THE ECOSYSTEM FOR EFFECTIVE MANAGEMENT & GROWTH

DR. GOVIND RAO

ISBN
Paperback 979-8-89322-961-5
Hardcase 979-8-89446-690-3

DEDICATION

This book is wholeheartedly dedicated to the extraordinary and multifaceted channel partners and their diligent teams who have had a profound impact on my professional journey. Over the years, I have had the privilege of working closely with these remarkable individuals, and their unwavering commitment, adaptability, and resilience have been a constant source of inspiration and learning.

Through the highs and lows of navigating the complex landscape of channel partnerships, these exceptional professionals have demonstrated an unparalleled level of tenacity and determination. They have consistently risen to the challenges posed by ever-changing market dynamics, technological advancements, and shifting customer preferences, always finding innovative ways to overcome obstacles and seize new opportunities.

The knowledge, skills, and expertise that these channel partners bring to the table have been invaluable in driving growth, fostering innovation, and delivering value to customers.

Working closely with these channel partners has been a transformative experience, both personally and professionally.

"The Channel Conundrum – Navigating the Ecosystem for Effective Management and Growth" is a tribute to the collective wisdom, experiences, and insights I have

garnered through my interactions with these remarkable channel partners.

Thank you for being an integral part of my journey, for sharing your knowledge and experiences, and for consistently pushing the boundaries of what is possible in channel partnerships. May your success continue to soar and may your passion for success never waver.

With heartfelt appreciation and respect,

Dr. Govind Rao

CONTENTS

Former Founding Managing Director Vodafone Fiji Ltd

Deputy Chairman Fiji Airways Ltd

Chairman of Fiji Directories Ltd

Aslam is a highly experienced and seasoned telecommunication executive who has been the founding Managing Director of Vodafone Fiji Limited. Aslam brings significant CEO experience of over 20+ years to the role, having seen three coups during his working life. He is personable and team-oriented, down to earth, and he is known for his customer service focus and for living the "Vodafone Way" and Vodafone culture under his leadership, Vodafone Fiji Ltd won several prestigious awards such as the President's Award [Malcom Bridge equivalent in Fiji] a record three-time and Fiji Quality awards three times.

He has built a brand reputation for Vodafone and maintained its number-one market position despite stiff competition from his rivals.

Aslam never retires; while he has stepped down from His role as Managing Director at Vodafone Fiji Ltd, he now continues to serve in non-executive roles on the Fiji Airways Board of Directors as Deputy Chairman and chairman of audit subcommittee and as Chairman of Fiji Directories Ltd [yellow pages].

Foreword

I am pleased to introduce you to *The Channel Conundrum – Navigating the Ecosystem for Effective Management and Growth*. In this comprehensive guide, author Dr Govind Rao provides invaluable insights into the complex world of channel sales, drawing upon his extensive experience and expertise in the field.

Navigating the Channels

Channel management is a multifaceted discipline that encompasses building, developing, measuring, managing, and maintaining sales channels. Whether you're a seasoned professional or new to the field, this book offers a holistic approach that covers a wide range of topics, from game theory to artificial intelligence, empowering you to make informed decisions and optimise your channel strategies.

The Art of Channel Execution

As you delve into these pages, you'll discover proven strategies for becoming a profitable and effective channel player. Govind Rao shares practical advice on avoiding common pitfalls and maximising your effectiveness in channel management execution. Whether you're dealing with distributors, retailers, or online platforms, *The Channel Conundrum – Navigating the Ecosystem for Effective Management and Growth* equips you with the tools and knowledge you need to navigate the intricacies of channel relationships and drive success.

A Forward-Looking Perspective

What sets this book apart is its forward-looking perspective. It goes beyond traditional channel models and explores emerging technologies and trends that are shaping the future of channel management. From understanding evolving customer behaviours to leveraging data analytics, *The Channel Conundrum* prepares you to thrive in a dynamic and rapidly changing marketplace.

About the Author

Dr. Govind Rao brings over 30 years of experience in marketing management, sales, and business consulting to this book. His deep industry knowledge and practical insights shine through these pages, making *The Channel Conundrum* an essential resource for anyone involved in channel sales, from channel managers and sales executives to entrepreneurs and business leaders.

A Valuable Resource

Whether you're looking to optimise your existing channel strategies, expand into new markets, or navigate the challenges of digital transformation, this book is a valuable resource that will guide you every step of the way. It offers a perfect blend of theoretical concepts and practical applications, enabling you to develop a comprehensive understanding of channel management and apply it to your specific business context.

An Invitation to Succeed

I invite you to embark on a transformative journey through the pages *The Channel Conundrum* Let Govind Rao's insights and guidance empower you to navigate the intricate channels of success, forge strong partnerships, and achieve your business objectives. May this book be your trusted companion as you explore the exciting world of channel management and unlock new opportunities for growth and profitability.

Warm regards,

Aslam Khan

Ayman El Dessouky BSc. MBA.

Chairman Tamweel Investments Holding. CEO/ MD/Board Member

Business leader, Senior Executive and Entrepreneur with +30 years of experience with global companies in the technology, telecommunications, and financial services industries. He worked with IBM and Vodafone in local, regional, and global positions for over 15 years.

With a proven record in delivering results, driving growth, and taking market challengers to market leadership in different markets across Europe, the Middle East, and North Africa. A senior executive with strong expertise in General Management, Corporate and Commercial Strategy, Mergers and Acquisitions, Large Operations Management, Company turn-around and large P&L management. Co-founder, Board Member, and partner in several successful companies.

FOREWORD

Channel Management has been a lifelong passion of mine, playing a pivotal role in my career across various positions at esteemed companies such as IBM, Vodafone, and e&. Throughout my professional journey, I have witnessed firsthand the transformative power of effective channel management in driving business success.

In today's dynamic and fiercely competitive business landscape, where markets are constantly evolving, and consumer preferences are shifting at an unprecedented pace, the importance of channel management cannot be overstated. As businesses navigate through a complex web of distribution channels to reach their target audiences, the ability to strategically orchestrate and optimize these channels has emerged as a critical differentiator.

My path has intersected with the author's journey in several professional capacities, where channel management was at the heart of our shared achievements. Dr. Govind's expertise in this field has been forged through extensive hands-on experience across multiple global corporations, where he has consistently demonstrated his ability to drive growth and optimize channel performance. This book serves as a comprehensive guide to the intricacies of channel management, offering invaluable insights, proven strategies, and best practices for maximizing channel effectiveness and driving sustainable growth. Drawing upon years of collective experience and deep expertise, the author provides a clear roadmap for navigating the complexities of channel ecosystems, from understanding the nuances of channel dynamics to forging strategic partnerships that unlock new opportunities.

Through a combination of real-world examples, case studies, and practical advice, this book equips readers with the tools and knowledge they need to build and manage a strong, resilient, and successful channel ecosystem. The author's approach is grounded in a deep understanding of the challenges and opportunities that businesses face in today's rapidly evolving marketplace and offers actionable insights that can be immediately applied to drive results.

Whether you are a seasoned channel manager looking to refine your approach and stay ahead of the curve or a newcomer seeking to grasp the fundamental principles of effective channel management, this book serves as an indispensable resource. It demystifies complex concepts, provides a clear framework for success, and offers a wealth of practical guidance that can be adapted to suit the unique needs of your organization.

I commend the author for his unwavering dedication to sharing his expertise and insights through this book. His passion for channel management shines through on every page, and his commitment to empowering others with the knowledge and tools they need to succeed is truly commendable.

I am confident that this book will become a treasured resource for channel managers, business leaders, and anyone seeking to unlock the full potential of their distribution channels. It is a must-read for anyone looking to stay ahead in today's competitive landscape and drive sustainable growth through effective channel management.

Ayman I. Eldessouky

CEO & MD Basata Investments Holding

Chairman Tamweel Investments Holding

John C Lincoln

Global B2B Leader

John C. Lincoln is an accomplished global commercial and operations executive with over four decades of experience in steering major telecommunications, cloud, digital service providers, and B2B/B2C organisations across numerous continents.

He boasts an impressive history of managing Profit & Loss statements for businesses generating incremental revenue of over US$1 billion. John's leadership extends to overseeing expansive teams of more than 1,000 individuals, where he fosters a culture of redefining success and implementing bold strategic initiatives to secure market dominance. As a seasoned senior leader, including roles as Chief Commercial Officer and Chief Business Officer, John excels in scaling businesses with constrained resources and achieving double-digit revenue growth in both emerging and established market scenarios.

His expertise spans strategic marketing, product development, B2B sales, customer service, operations, service implementation, collections, business expansion, and mergers & acquisitions. John's global operational insights are drawn from his experience in leading substantial teams across the USA, Japan, the United Kingdom, India, the UAE, Saudi Arabia, and Malaysia.

Having served in top executive positions at prominent global brands, including telecommunications giants like Vodafone, Etisalat (now E&), SoftBank, Fidelity, AT&T, AirTel, du, and Mobily, John is recognised for his transformative leadership and capacity to foster growth. He is acknowledged as a pivotal figure and advocate for transformational shifts in four major telecom entities – one each in Japan and Saudi Arabia and two in the UAE.

John is also a published author, having penned *Connect the Dots - A Playbook to Help You Connect to Your Customer and Profits*, a business guide aimed at small and medium enterprise owners. Additionally, he is featured as one of four main protagonists in a Harvard Business School case study, which celebrated that team's transformational leadership and John's leadership in. churn management strategies during a critical turnaround phase for a company in Japan.

Dedicated to achieving results and leading transformational change, John is committed to propelling business success in any B2B-focused or turnaround scenario.

FOREWORD

In the rapidly evolving, challenging, and complex commercial world of B2B, the art and science of channel management stand as a critical and pivotal element that can make or break an enterprise's market share and profitability.

It is with great enthusiasm that I am happy to introduce *The Channel Conundrum*, authored by Govind Rao, a true expert in the channel strategy and execution space.

During my various B2B unit leadership tenures and particularly as the Senior Vice President of Small and Medium Businesses at Etisalat (now e&) in the UAE, I had the privilege of witnessing Govind's extraordinary talent firsthand as the Vice President of Channel Management on my team.

Govind's brilliant channel insights, strategies and tactics were instrumental in catapulting our telecom organisation from a laggard in the SMB space to the forefront as the unequivocal market share leader in the country! These channel strategies and tactics helped us secure billions in incremental revenue and establish us as an unbeatable and dominant force against our competitors.

Govind Rao embodies a rare confluence of deep theoretical knowledge, extensive practical experience, and groundbreaking insights into the nuances of channel management. This book is a testament to his mastery, encapsulating the wisdom gleaned from his remarkable global career in the B2B space.

This book offers a comprehensive exploration of channel management that is unparalleled in its depth and breadth, covering essential topics such as channel design, incentive design, channel economics, and much more.

The chapters within this book delve into the critical aspects of B2B channel management, from the foundational principles outlined in the Introduction to Channel Management through the intricate strategies involved in Designing a Channel Strategy and Managing Partnerships to the advanced topics discussed in the sections on Technology in Channel Management and Legal and Ethical Considerations.

Each section is meticulously crafted to provide readers with a holistic understanding of the subject matter, blending theoretical insights with practical applications.

One of the most compelling aspects of Govind's approach is his adeptness at incentive design and channel economics, which are crucial for attracting & motivating channel partners. I encourage the readers to pay special attention to this critical factor as this had one of the biggest impacts on optimising channel performance.

His strategies for developing robust channel designs that align with business goals and the dynamic needs of stakeholders are particularly enlightening.

Furthermore, Govind's exploration of channel technology, including the use of data analytics for channel optimisation, reflects his forward-thinking approach and commitment to leveraging cutting-edge tools to enhance channel effectiveness.

Govind's contributions have not only reshaped our company's trajectory but have also set new standards for excellence in channel management. His innovative strategies for overcoming competition and achieving market dominance are articulated with clarity and precision in this book, serving as an invaluable resource for professionals seeking to replicate the success that we had then.

The Channel Conundrum is more than a guide; it is an inspiration for channel management professionals and business leaders alike. Govind's unique blend of skills and insights, combined with his successful track record, positions this book as an essential read for anyone looking to excel in the complex world of B2B channel management.

As you embark on the journey through these pages, be prepared to be enlightened, inspired, and equipped with the knowledge and tools necessary to master the art of channel management. Govind Rao's legacy of success is now yours to build upon.

John Lincoln

Ramakrishna Movva (Ramki) Ph.D.

Founder & CEO

Chrysalis Consulting Solutions

Dr. Ramakrishna Movva is a firm believer that all transformations at an organisational or individual level must be intrinsically driven. He has over 30 years of experience leading organisational and leadership transformation initiatives.

Before founding Chrysalis Consulting Solutions, he was the Executive VP & Head of Strategic HR and Organisational Capabilities at Emirates NBD Bank in Dubai, UAE.

He also worked as an HR consulting lead at Price Waterhouse and performed various HR management roles at Unilever.

He holds a doctoral degree from the California Institute of Integral Studies, USA, a post-graduate diploma in Occupational Psychology from the University of Surrey, UK, and a master's degree in HR from the Tata Institute of Social Sciences, India.

Dr. Ramakrishna Movva is also an International Coach Federation-certified leadership and team coach. I enjoy participating in regional HR conferences as a keynote speaker and a panellist.

FOREWORD

I am privileged to write this foreword for Dr Govind Rao's insightful and compelling book, *The Channel Conundrum*. As someone who has dedicated my career to organisational and leadership transformations, I find this book powerfully illustrating the ethos and dynamics of the channel partner ecosystem.

Dr. Govind draws upon his extensive experience and keen understanding of channel management to present a compelling case for unravelling its complex terrain. Through engaging case studies, profound insights, and practical guidance, he illustrates how organisations and business leaders can spot and leverage transformative opportunities in channel management to deliver a world-class customer experience and sales growth. This book is an invaluable guide for business leaders who wish to pursue this exciting journey.

With wisdom, compassion, and a grounding in real-world experience, Dr Govind leads readers to a deeper understanding of channel dynamics and provides them with the tools and frameworks needed to drive growth in channel sales while embracing a customer-centric mindset. Dr Govind's holistic approach addresses the challenges and opportunities in channel management. The ripple effects of the guiding principles highlighted in the book will be felt across teams, organisations, and channel partner communities. I am confident that this book will profoundly impact organisations and business leaders who drive customer experience and channel sales.

It is an honour to recommend this groundbreaking book, which I am confident will catalyse robust growth and success in the channel partner ecosystem.

Dr. Ramakrishna Movva

PREFACE

In today's rapidly evolving business landscape, mastering the intricacies of channel management has become an imperative for organisations seeking to thrive amidst fierce competition and shifting customer preferences. *The Channel Conundrum- Navigating the Ecosystem for Effective Management and Growth* emerges as an indispensable resource, meticulously crafted to guide practitioners, executives, and scholars through the complex terrain of channel management.

This comprehensive volume ventures beyond the realm of conventional wisdom, delving into the core principles, strategic imperatives, and practical nuances that underpin effective channel management. By seamlessly blending theoretical insights with real-world case studies and actionable strategies, *The Channel Conundrum* equips readers with the tools and knowledge necessary to confidently navigate the intricate web of distribution channels.

At its core, this book serves as a guiding light, illuminating the strategic decisions, operational challenges, and transformative opportunities that define the channel management landscape. Each chapter has been carefully curated to provide a holistic perspective, enabling readers to grasp the dynamics of channel relationships, partner collaboration, and technological disruption while empowering them to leverage distribution channels as strategic assets for growth and competitive advantage.

As you embark on this journey through the pages of *The Channel Conundrum*, prepare to uncover a treasure trove of insights and practical wisdom. Whether you are a seasoned executive aiming to optimise your organisation's distribution strategies or an aspiring professional seeking to deepen your understanding of marketing and distribution, this book will serve as your trusted companion, guiding you towards the pinnacle of channel management excellence.

Join us on this exploratory voyage through the channels of commerce as we navigate the tides of market dynamics, charting a course towards sustainable growth, market leadership, and enduring success.

Armed with the knowledge and strategic foresight imparted by *The Channel Conundrum*, you will be well-equipped to tackle the complexities of channel management with clarity, purpose, and unwavering determination.

As you set sail on this transformative journey, let *The Channel Conundrum* be your north star, illuminating the path towards mastering the art and science of channel management. Embrace the insights within these pages and unlock the full potential of your distribution channels, propelling your organisation towards new horizons of success in an ever-changing business world.

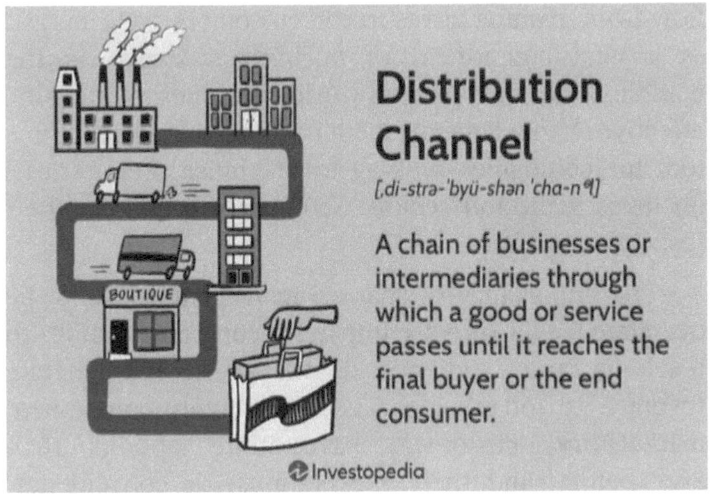

CHAPTER 1

INTRODUCTION TO CHANNEL MANAGEMENT

Introduction

In the dynamic and ever-evolving landscape of modern business, companies face the critical challenge of achieving sustainable growth and maintaining market relevance. To succeed in this complex environment, organisations must skilfully navigate the intricate web of distribution channels. Channel management, the strategic process of overseeing and optimising the various pathways through which products and services flow from manufacturers to end customers, has emerged as a vital component of business strategy. As the complexity of the business world continues to intensify, effective channel management becomes an indispensable tool for companies seeking to maximise their returns on investment and secure a competitive edge in their respective markets.

The importance of channel management cannot be overstated, as it directly impacts a company's ability to reach its target audience, deliver value, and generate revenue. In today's globalised and highly competitive marketplace, customers have more options than ever before, and their expectations for convenience, accessibility, and personalised experiences are at an all-time high. To meet these demands and differentiate themselves from competitors, companies must develop sophisticated channel strategies that leverage the strengths of various distribution partners, such as wholesalers, retailers, e-commerce platforms, and logistics providers. By carefully selecting, managing, and optimising these partnerships, organisations can expand their market reach, improve customer satisfaction, and drive profitable growth.

However, the path to effective channel management is not without its challenges. Companies must navigate a myriad of complexities, including divergent partner goals, shifting market dynamics, technological disruptions, and regulatory constraints. To overcome these obstacles and unlock the full potential of their distribution networks, organisations must adopt a proactive, data-driven, and customer-centric approach to channel management. This requires a deep understanding of customer needs and preferences, a commitment to continuous improvement, and a willingness to adapt to changing market conditions.

In the following pages, we will delve into the fundamental concepts, strategies, and best practices of channel management. We will explore the various types of distribution channels, the key components of effective channel design, and the critical success factors for building and maintaining strong partnerships. By the end of this chapter, readers will have a comprehensive understanding of how to develop and execute a robust channel management strategy that drives business success in today's complex and competitive marketplace.

Introduction (Continued)

This chapter aims to provide a comprehensive exploration of channel management, delving into its multifaceted dimensions and illuminating its pivotal role in shaping organisational success. By embarking on this in-depth analysis, we will unravel the complexities of channel management and shed light on its strategic significance. Through a meticulous examination of its various aspects, we will gain valuable insights into how companies can leverage channel management to optimise their distribution networks, enhance customer reach, and drive sustainable growth. Understanding the intricacies of channel management is essential for business leaders and decision-makers who seek to navigate the challenges of the modern business landscape and position their organisations for long-term success.

To fully appreciate the importance of channel management, it is essential to consider its far-reaching impact on various aspects of business operations. Effective channel management enables companies to optimise their supply chain processes, reducing costs, improving efficiency, and ensuring the timely delivery of products to customers. By collaborating closely with distribution partners, organisations can streamline logistics, minimise inventory holding costs, and respond quickly to fluctuations in demand. Moreover, well-managed channels contribute to enhanced brand visibility and customer loyalty, as companies can ensure consistent messaging, pricing, and service quality across all touchpoints.

Another critical aspect of channel management is its role in fostering innovation and driving market responsiveness. By leveraging the insights, expertise, and market knowledge of distribution partners, companies can gain valuable feedback on customer preferences, emerging trends, and competitive dynamics. This information can inform product development, marketing strategies, and customer engagement initiatives, enabling organisations to stay ahead of the curve and seize new growth opportunities. Furthermore, effective channel management allows companies to experiment with new distribution models, such as direct-to-customer sales or subscription-based services, to adapt to changing customer behaviours and market conditions.

Throughout this chapter, we will explore the various strategies and techniques that companies can employ to master the art of channel management. We will discuss the importance of developing a clear and coherent channel strategy that aligns with overall business objectives and target customer segments. We will also examine the key considerations for selecting and onboarding distribution partners, including the evaluation of their capabilities, alignment of incentives, and establishment of performance metrics. Additionally, we will delve into the critical aspects of partner relationship management, including effective communication, conflict resolution, and continuous performance improvement.

By the end of this chapter, readers will have a deep appreciation for the strategic importance of channel management and a practical understanding of how to develop and execute a successful channel strategy. Armed with this knowledge, business leaders and decision-makers will be well-equipped to navigate the complexities of the modern business landscape, forge strong partnerships, and drive sustainable growth in an increasingly competitive and dynamic marketplace.

Defining Channels

In the realm of commerce, channels serve as the vital arteries through which goods and services flow from producers to customers. These conduits form the backbone of any economy, facilitating the efficient distribution of products and the satisfaction of customer demands. Channels encompass a wide range of intermediaries, including wholesalers, retailers, distributors, and e-commerce platforms, each playing a crucial role in the supply chain. By bridging the gap between manufacturers and end-users, channels enable businesses to extend their reach, tap into new markets, and deliver value to their target audience. Understanding the nature and function of channels is essential for companies seeking to optimise their distribution strategies and ensure the smooth flow of their offerings to the right customers at the right time.

At its core, a distribution channel is a network of organisations that work together to make a product or service available to the end customer. These organisations can include manufacturers, wholesalers, distributors, retailers, and various other intermediaries. Each member of the channel plays a specific role in the distribution process, adding value through functions such as transportation, storage, packaging, marketing, and customer service. The structure and complexity of a distribution channel can vary greatly depending on the nature of the product, the target market, and the company's overall business strategy.

One of the primary functions of distribution channels is to bridge the gap between production and consumption. Manufacturers often lack the resources, expertise, or market presence to effectively reach and serve end customers directly. By partnering with intermediaries who specialise in distribution, companies can focus on their core competencies of product development and production, while leveraging the capabilities and networks of their channel partners to efficiently deliver their offerings to the market. This division of labour allows for greater efficiency, economies of scale, and market penetration.

Another essential role of distribution channels is to provide value-added services that enhance the customer experience and differentiate a company's offerings from competitors. These services can include product customisation, installation, training, technical support, and after-sales service. By working closely with channel partners who have direct contact with customers, companies can gain valuable insights into customer needs, preferences, and behaviours. This information can inform product development, marketing strategies, and customer engagement initiatives, enabling companies to continuously improve their offerings and stay ahead of the competition.

In today's digital age, the concept of distribution channels has evolved to include e-commerce platforms and online marketplaces. These digital channels have revolutionised the way companies reach and serve customers, offering unparalleled convenience, accessibility, and personalisation. Online channels allow companies to transcend geographic boundaries, reach a global audience, and gather rich data on customer behaviour and preferences. However, managing these digital channels effectively requires a different set of skills and strategies compared to traditional brick-and-mortar distribution.

As companies navigate the complexities of channel management, it is essential to recognise the unique characteristics and requirements of each type of channel. Wholesalers, for example, typically purchase products in bulk from manufacturers and resell them to retailers or other businesses. They play a critical role in providing economies of scale, managing inventory, and extending credit to smaller buyers. Retailers, on the other hand, are the final link in the distribution chain, selling products directly to end customers. They focus on creating compelling in-store experiences, managing product assortments, and building brand loyalty.

Understanding the distinct roles and value propositions of each channel member is crucial for developing effective channel strategies and partnerships. Companies must carefully evaluate the strengths, weaknesses, and potential synergies of each channel option, taking into account factors such as market coverage, cost efficiency, control over the customer experience, and alignment with overall business objectives. By designing and managing a well-balanced portfolio of channels, companies can optimise their distribution networks, reach the right customers through the most appropriate channels, and maximise their return on investment.

Distribution channels play a vital role in connecting producers with end customers and facilitating the efficient flow of goods and services in the economy. By understanding the nature and function of various types of channels, companies can develop effective strategies for reaching and serving their target markets while leveraging the capabilities and expertise of their channel partners. As the business landscape continues to evolve, with the rise of digital channels and changing customer behaviours, mastering the art of channel management has become more critical than ever for companies seeking to achieve sustainable growth and competitive advantage.

Significance of Channel Management

Channel management stands as a cornerstone of a company's business strategy, exerting a profound influence on multiple aspects of its operations. Effective channel management enables organisations to expand their market reach, ensuring that their products and services are accessible to a broader customer base. By strategically selecting and managing distribution partners, companies can penetrate new geographic regions, target specific customer segments, and establish a strong presence in key markets. Moreover, channel management plays a vital role in enhancing customer accessibility, allowing businesses to deliver their offerings through the most convenient and preferred channels for their target audience. By aligning their distribution strategies with customer preferences and behaviours, companies can improve customer satisfaction and foster long-term loyalty. Additionally, channel management contributes to operational efficiency by streamlining logistics, optimising inventory management, and reducing distribution costs. By leveraging the expertise and resources of channel partners, organisations can achieve economies of scale, improve supply chain agility, and enhance overall operational performance. Furthermore, effective channel management has a direct impact on revenue generation, as it enables companies to maximise sales opportunities, capture market share, and drive profitable growth. By carefully selecting and nurturing relationships with high-performing channel partners, businesses can unlock new revenue streams, expand their customer base, and increase their bottom line.

One of the primary objectives of channel management is to ensure that a company's products or services are readily available to customers in the right place, at the right time, and in the right quantity. This requires a deep understanding of customer needs, preferences, and purchasing behaviours, as well as a strategic approach to channel design and partner selection. By conducting thorough market research and segmenting customers based on their unique characteristics and requirements, companies can develop targeted channel strategies that align with the needs of specific customer groups. This enables organisations to optimise their distribution networks, minimise channel conflict, and ensure that each partner is well-positioned to serve its designated market segment effectively.

Another critical aspect of channel management is the ability to adapt to changing market dynamics and customer expectations. In today's fast-paced and highly competitive business environment, companies must be agile and responsive to shifts in customer behaviour, technological advancements, and industry trends. Effective channel management allows organisations to quickly adjust their distribution strategies, modify their product offerings, and explore new channels to meet evolving customer demands. By fostering close collaboration and open communication with channel partners, companies can gain valuable insights into market trends, customer feedback, and competitive activities. This information can inform strategic decision-making, enable proactive problem-solving, and drive continuous improvement across the distribution network.

Moreover, channel management plays a crucial role in building and maintaining strong relationships with distribution partners. These partnerships are built on a foundation of trust, mutual benefit, and shared goals. By investing in partner enablement programmes, providing comprehensive training and support, and establishing clear performance metrics and incentives, companies can empower their channel partners to excel in their roles and deliver exceptional value to customers. Regular communication, joint planning sessions, and performance reviews help to align partner activities with corporate objectives, identify areas for improvement, and foster a culture of continuous learning and growth. By nurturing these relationships and treating channel partners as true extensions of their own organisations, companies can create a collaborative ecosystem that drives innovation, efficiency, and customer satisfaction.

Effective channel management also requires a data-driven approach to decision-making and performance optimisation. With the proliferation of digital technologies and the increasing availability of customer and sales data, companies have unprecedented opportunities to gain insights into channel performance, partner effectiveness, and customer behaviour. By leveraging advanced analytics tools and techniques, organisations can monitor key performance indicators (KPIs), identify trends and patterns, and make informed decisions to optimise their distribution strategies. This data-driven approach enables companies to allocate resources more effectively, target high-potential partners and markets, and continuously refine their channel management practices based on real-world performance metrics.

Furthermore, channel management is essential for protecting a company's brand reputation and ensuring consistent customer experiences across all touchpoints.

In a multi-channel environment, where customers interact with a brand through various online and offline channels, maintaining a cohesive brand identity and delivering a seamless customer journey is paramount. Effective channel management helps to establish clear brand guidelines, communication protocols, and quality standards that all partners must adhere to. By monitoring partner performance, providing regular feedback and support, and taking swift action to address any issues or inconsistencies, companies can safeguard their brand integrity and build customer trust and loyalty.

Channel management is a critical component of a company's overall business strategy, influencing its ability to reach and serve customers effectively, drive operational efficiency, and generate sustainable growth. By developing a deep understanding of customer needs, fostering strong partnerships, leveraging data-driven insights, and ensuring brand consistency, companies can optimise their distribution networks and create a powerful competitive advantage. As the business landscape continues to evolve, with the emergence of new channels, technologies, and customer expectations, mastering the art of channel management will remain a key determinant of organisational success in the years to come.

Significance of Channel Management (Continued)

Effective channel management plays a crucial role in fostering mutually beneficial relationships between companies and their channel partners. By investing in partner relationship management, organisations can cultivate strong, collaborative partnerships built on trust and aligned interests. Through open communication, shared goals, and joint problem-solving, companies and their channel partners can work together to overcome challenges, seize opportunities, and drive mutual success. By providing channel partners with the necessary support, resources, and incentives, businesses can empower them to effectively promote and sell their products while also ensuring consistent brand representation and customer experience across all touchpoints. Moreover, effective channel management enables companies to leverage the market knowledge, local expertise, and customer relationships of their partners, gaining valuable insights into regional preferences, competitive dynamics, and emerging trends. By fostering a spirit of collaboration and mutual growth, organisations can build long-term, sustainable partnerships that deliver value to all stakeholders involved.

One of the key elements of successful partner relationship management is the establishment of clear expectations and performance metrics. By setting well-defined goals, roles, and responsibilities for each channel partner, companies can ensure that everyone is working towards common objectives and that their efforts are aligned with the overall business strategy. This includes defining sales targets, market share goals, customer satisfaction measures, and other relevant KPIs that reflect the unique contributions and value proposition of each partner. Regular performance reviews and feedback sessions help to track progress, identify areas for improvement, and celebrate successes, fostering a culture of accountability and continuous learning.

Another critical aspect of partner relationship management is the provision of comprehensive training and support programmes. Channel partners often serve as the face of a company to its customers, and their knowledge, skills, and attitudes can significantly impact the customer experience and brand perception. By investing in training initiatives that cover product features, sales techniques, customer service best practices, and brand guidelines, companies can equip their partners with the tools and confidence they need to excel in their roles. Additionally, providing ongoing support through dedicated account managers, technical experts, and marketing resources helps to address any challenges or questions that partners may encounter, ensuring that they feel valued and

empowered to succeed.

Effective channel management also involves the creation of incentive and reward programmes that motivate partners to perform at their best. These programmes can include sales commissions, volume discounts, performance bonuses, and other financial incentives that align partner interests with those of the company. Non-financial rewards, such as exclusive training opportunities, joint marketing initiatives, and public recognition, can also play a powerful role in fostering partner loyalty and engagement. By designing incentive structures that are fair, transparent, and aligned with strategic objectives, companies can encourage partners to go above and beyond in their efforts to promote and sell products while also ensuring that their own profitability and growth goals are met.

Moreover, effective partner relationship management requires a proactive approach to conflict resolution and problem-solving. In any multi-channel environment, there is the potential for conflicts to arise due to competing interests, resource constraints, or communication breakdowns. By establishing clear protocols for identifying, escalating, and resolving conflicts in a timely and constructive manner, companies can minimise the impact of these issues on partner relationships and overall channel performance. This may involve regular check-ins with partners to discuss concerns and challenges, as well as the development of joint problem-solving teams that bring together representatives from both the company and its partners to collaborate on solutions.

Another key aspect of partner relationship management is the sharing of information and best practices across the channel network. By creating forums for partners to exchange ideas, share success stories, and learn from each other's experiences, companies can foster a sense of community and collaboration that benefits the entire ecosystem. This can include regular partner conferences, online knowledge-sharing platforms, and peer-to-peer mentoring programmes that encourage partners to support and learn from one another. By facilitating the flow of information and expertise across the network, companies can accelerate innovation, drive efficiencies, and create a more agile and responsive channel system.

Finally, effective partner relationship management requires a long-term perspective and a commitment to continuous improvement. Building strong, sustainable partnerships takes time, effort, and patience, and companies must be willing to invest in these relationships for the long haul. This means regularly assessing partner performance and satisfaction, seeking feedback and input from partners on how to improve processes and programmes, and making necessary adjustments to keep the partnership aligned with evolving business needs and market conditions. By approaching partner relationship management as an ongoing, iterative process rather than a one-time event, companies can create a foundation of trust, mutual respect, and shared success that will serve them well for years to come.

Effective channel management is essential for building and maintaining strong, collaborative relationships with channel partners. By establishing clear expectations, providing comprehensive training and support, creating motivating incentive programmes, fostering open communication and problem-solving, and taking a long-term perspective, companies can unlock the full potential of their partnerships and drive mutual success.

Key Components of Channel Management

Developing a robust channel strategy is a critical component of effective channel management. The process begins with a thorough evaluation of market dynamics, including an analysis of customer needs, competitive landscape, and industry trends. By understanding the unique characteristics and requirements of their target markets, companies can make informed decisions about the most suitable distribution channels to employ. This involves identifying and segmenting target customer groups based on their preferences, behaviours, and purchasing patterns, allowing organisations to tailor their channel strategies to specific customer segments. Once the target markets are identified, companies must assess the various channel options available, weighing the strengths, weaknesses, and potential synergies of each alternative. This evaluation takes into account factors such as reach, cost, control, flexibility, and alignment with overall business objectives. Based on this comprehensive analysis, companies can then design and implement distribution plans that optimise channel performance, ensure efficient product flow, and deliver value to customers. These plans may involve a mix of direct and indirect channels, such as owned retail stores, e-commerce platforms, distributors, wholesalers, and resellers, each serving specific roles in the overall distribution network. The ultimate goal is to establish a channel strategy that aligns with the company's business objectives, leverages the unique strengths of each channel partner, and effectively meets the needs and preferences of target customers in the most efficient and profitable manner.

Another key component of effective channel management is the development of a comprehensive partner onboarding and enablement programme. Once the right channel partners have been identified and selected, it is essential to provide them with the necessary tools, resources, and support to succeed in their roles. This includes product training, sales and marketing materials, technical support, and access to customer data and insights. By investing in partner enablement from the outset, companies can ensure that their channel partners are well-equipped to represent their brand, communicate their value proposition, and deliver exceptional customer experiences. Moreover, a structured onboarding process helps to establish clear expectations, performance metrics, and communication protocols, setting the stage for a productive and mutually beneficial partnership.

Effective channel management also requires a robust performance management system that tracks and measures the success of each channel partner. This involves defining clear KPIs that align with the company's overall business objectives and the specific goals of each channel. These metrics may include sales volume, market share, customer acquisition and retention rates, profitability, and customer satisfaction scores. By regularly monitoring and analysing these KPIs, companies can gain valuable insights into the effectiveness of their channel strategies, identify areas for improvement, and make data-driven decisions to optimise performance. Performance management also includes providing regular feedback and coaching to channel partners, celebrating successes, and addressing any issues or challenges in a timely and constructive manner.

Another critical component of channel management is the development of a comprehensive partner incentive and reward programme. These programmes are designed to motivate and encourage channel partners to perform at their best, driving sales, market share, and customer satisfaction. Incentives can take many forms, including volume discounts, sales commissions, performance bonuses, and non-financial rewards such as exclusive training opportunities or marketing support. The key is to design incentive structures that are aligned with the company's overall business objectives, are fair and transparent, and provide meaningful rewards for partner performance. By creating a compelling value proposition for channel partners and recognising their contributions to the company's success, organisations can foster a sense of loyalty, engagement, and shared purpose that drives long-term growth and profitability.

Finally, effective channel management requires a strong focus on continuous improvement and innovation. As market conditions, customer preferences, and competitive dynamics evolve, companies must be able to adapt and refine their channel strategies to stay ahead of the curve. This involves regularly assessing the performance of each channel, seeking feedback and input from partners and customers, and identifying opportunities for optimisation and growth. By fostering a culture of innovation and experimentation within the channel network, companies can encourage partners to develop new ideas, test new approaches, and share best practices that benefit the entire ecosystem. Moreover, by staying attuned to emerging trends and technologies, such as digital transformation, omnichannel retailing, and data analytics, organisations can proactively evolve their channel strategies to meet the changing needs and expectations of their customers.

Effective channel management requires a multifaceted approach that encompasses strategic planning, partner enablement, performance management, incentive design, and continuous improvement. By mastering these key components, companies can build strong, collaborative relationships with their channel partners, optimise their distribution networks, and drive sustainable growth and profitability in an increasingly complex and competitive business landscape.

Key Components of Channel Management (Continued)

Partner relationship management is another critical component of effective channel management. Building strong, sustainable partnerships with channel partners is essential for driving mutual value creation and long-term business growth. Companies must invest time and resources in nurturing these relationships, fostering open communication, trust, and alignment of interests. This involves establishing clear expectations, defining roles and responsibilities, and setting shared goals and objectives. Regular engagement and collaboration with channel partners help to identify areas for improvement, resolve conflicts, and explore new opportunities for growth. By providing partners with the necessary training, support, and resources, companies can empower them to effectively represent their brands, deliver exceptional customer experiences, and drive sales. Moreover, implementing incentive programmes, performance metrics, and recognition systems can motivate partners to excel and align their efforts with the company's strategic priorities. Effective partner relationship management also involves continuously monitoring and evaluating partner performance, providing feedback and coaching to help partners improve their capabilities and achieve their full potential. By cultivating a culture of mutual respect, transparency, and continuous improvement, companies can build long-lasting partnerships that generate value for all parties involved and contribute to sustainable business success.

One of the key elements of successful partner relationship management is the establishment of a robust communication framework. Clear, consistent, and timely communication is essential for ensuring that all channel partners are aligned with the company's goals, strategies, and expectations. This includes regular updates on product launches, marketing campaigns, pricing changes, and other relevant information that impacts the channel. Moreover, creating open lines of communication that encourage two-way dialogue and feedback is crucial for fostering trust, collaboration, and continuous improvement. This can be achieved through a variety of channels, such as partner portals, newsletters, webinars, and face-to-face meetings, each serving specific purposes and catering to different partner preferences and needs.

Another critical aspect of partner relationship management is the development of joint business planning and goal-setting processes. By working collaboratively with channel partners to define shared objectives, strategies, and tactics, companies can ensure that everyone is working towards common goals and that resources are allocated effectively. This involves conducting regular business reviews, assessing market opportunities and challenges, and adjusting plans as needed based on performance and feedback. Joint business planning also helps to identify areas where the company can provide additional support or resources to help partners succeed, such as co-marketing funds, lead generation programmes, or technical training.

Effective partner relationship management also requires a strong focus on partner enablement and development. Investing in comprehensive training and certification programmes that help partners acquire the knowledge, skills, and competencies they need to effectively sell and support the company's products and services is essential for driving channel success. This includes product training, sales and negotiation skills, customer service best practices, and technical support. Moreover, providing partners with access to a wide range of marketing and sales resources, such as product collateral, case studies, demo scripts, and competitive intelligence, can help them to effectively communicate the value proposition and differentiate the company's offerings in the market.

Another key element of partner relationship management is the development of a fair and transparent performance management system. Setting clear, measurable, and achievable targets for each partner and regularly tracking and reporting on their progress is essential for ensuring that everyone is aligned and accountable for delivering results. This includes defining key performance indicators (KPIs) such as revenue growth, market share, customer satisfaction, and partner profitability, as well as providing regular feedback and coaching to help partners optimise their performance. Moreover, implementing a balanced scorecard approach that takes into account both quantitative and qualitative measures of partner success can help to create a more holistic and nuanced view of partner contributions and value.

Finally, effective partner relationship management requires a strong commitment to partner recognition and reward. Celebrating partner successes, acknowledging their contributions, and providing meaningful incentives and rewards for performance are essential for fostering a sense of loyalty, motivation, and engagement among channel partners. This can include financial incentives such as sales commissions, volume rebates, and performance bonuses, as well as non-financial rewards such as exclusive training opportunities, marketing support, and public recognition. By creating a compelling value proposition for partners and recognising their achievements, companies can create a virtuous cycle of performance and growth that benefits all parties involved.

Effective partner relationship management is a critical component of channel management that requires a multifaceted approach encompassing communication, joint planning, enablement, performance management, and recognition. By investing in these key areas and fostering strong, collaborative relationships with channel partners, companies can drive mutual value creation, long-term growth, and sustainable success in an increasingly complex and competitive business landscape.

Key Components of Channel Management (Continued)

Analysing performance data and identifying areas for improvement allows companies to refine their channel strategies, optimise resource allocation, and drive continuous improvements in channel performance. It is crucial for companies to engage in this process to enhance the efficiency and effectiveness of their channels.

One of the key steps in performance analysis is the establishment of a comprehensive data collection and reporting system. This involves defining clear metrics and key performance indicators (KPIs) that align with the company's overall business objectives and channel strategy. These metrics may include sales volume, market share, customer acquisition and retention rates, partner profitability, and customer satisfaction scores, among others. By regularly tracking and monitoring these KPIs, companies can gain a clear and objective view of channel performance, identify trends and patterns, and make data-driven decisions to optimise their strategies.

Another critical aspect of performance analysis is the use of advanced analytics tools and techniques to derive actionable insights from the data. This may involve leveraging business intelligence platforms, data visualisation tools, and machine learning algorithms to uncover hidden patterns, correlations, and opportunities for improvement. For example, by analysing sales data across different regions, customer segments, and product categories, companies can identify high-performing areas and best practices that can be replicated across the channel network. Similarly, by examining customer feedback and satisfaction scores, organisations can pinpoint areas where the customer experience can be enhanced and partner training and support can be improved.

Effective performance analysis also requires a collaborative approach that involves all stakeholders in the channel network. This includes regularly sharing performance data and insights with channel partners, soliciting their feedback and input, and working together to identify areas for improvement and develop action plans. By fostering a culture of transparency, accountability, and continuous learning, companies can create a shared sense of ownership and responsibility for driving channel success. Moreover, by involving partners in the performance improvement process, organisations can tap into their unique insights, expertise, and market knowledge to develop more effective and tailored strategies.

Another key element of performance analysis is the use of benchmarking and best practice sharing. By comparing channel performance against industry standards, competitor strategies, and internal benchmarks, companies can identify gaps and opportunities for improvement. This may involve conducting regular competitor analysis, attending industry events and conferences, and participating in benchmarking studies and surveys. Moreover, by fostering a culture of best practice sharing and knowledge transfer within the channel network, companies can accelerate the adoption of proven strategies and tactics and drive continuous improvement across the board.

Finally, effective performance analysis requires a strong focus on action planning and execution. Once areas for improvement have been identified and prioritised, companies must develop clear, measurable, and achievable action plans to address them. This may involve adjusting channel strategies, reallocating resources, providing additional training and support to partners, or implementing new technologies and processes. Moreover, by regularly monitoring progress against these action plans and adjusting course as needed, organisations can ensure that they are making tangible and sustainable improvements in channel performance over time.

Analysing performance data and identifying areas for improvement is a critical component of effective channel management. By establishing comprehensive data collection and reporting systems, leveraging advanced analytics tools and techniques, fostering collaboration and best practice sharing, and developing action-oriented improvement plans, companies can continuously refine their channel strategies, optimise resource allocation, and drive long-term growth and success. As the business landscape continues to evolve and become more complex, the ability to effectively analyse and act on channel performance data will be a key differentiator for organisations looking to stay ahead of the curve and maintain a competitive edge.

Key Components of Channel Management (Continued)

Proactive conflict management enables companies to address underlying issues, improve communication, and foster collaboration among channel partners, thereby enhancing the overall performance of the channel. It allows organisations to gain better control over their channel partnerships and achieve better results.

Conflict is an inherent part of any business relationship, and channel partnerships are no exception. Conflicts can arise due to a variety of factors, such as misaligned goals, competing priorities, resource constraints, or communication breakdowns. If left unaddressed, these conflicts can erode trust, damage relationships, and undermine the overall performance of the channel. Therefore, it is essential for companies to adopt a proactive and systematic approach to conflict management, one that focuses on prevention, early detection, and swift resolution.

One of the key elements of effective conflict management is the establishment of clear roles, responsibilities, and expectations for all parties involved in the channel partnership. This includes defining the scope of the relationship, setting performance targets and metrics, and establishing clear lines of communication and escalation. By setting a strong foundation for the partnership from the outset, companies can reduce the likelihood of misunderstandings and conflicts down the line. Moreover, by regularly reviewing and updating these agreements as the partnership evolves, organisations can ensure that everyone remains aligned and accountable.

Another critical aspect of conflict management is the development of a robust communication and feedback system. This involves establishing regular check-ins, performance reviews, and feedback sessions with channel partners to discuss progress, challenges, and opportunities for improvement. By fostering open, honest, and constructive dialogue, companies can identify potential issues early on and work collaboratively with partners to address them before they escalate into full-blown conflicts. Moreover, by actively listening to partner concerns and perspectives, organisations can gain valuable insights into market dynamics, customer needs, and competitive trends, which can inform strategic decision-making and drive continuous improvement.

Effective conflict management also requires a proactive approach to problem-solving and dispute resolution. This involves establishing clear protocols and processes for identifying, escalating, and resolving conflicts in a timely and fair manner. This may include the use of formal mediation or arbitration services, as well as the development of joint problem-solving teams that bring together representatives from both the company and its channel partners. By taking a collaborative and solutions-oriented approach to conflict resolution, companies can minimise the impact of disputes on the overall partnership and channel performance while also fostering a culture of trust, respect, and mutual benefit.

Another key element of conflict management is the use of data and analytics to identify patterns and root causes of conflicts. By regularly tracking and analysing data on partner performance, customer feedback, and market trends, companies can identify potential areas of friction or misalignment before they escalate into full-blown conflicts. Moreover, by using advanced analytics tools and techniques, such as predictive modelling and sentiment analysis, organisations can proactively identify and address potential issues before they impact the channel. This data-driven approach to conflict management can help companies make more informed decisions, allocate resources more effectively, and drive continuous improvement in channel performance over time.

Finally, effective conflict management requires a strong commitment to partner education and development. By investing in comprehensive training and development programmes that help partners acquire the skills, knowledge, and competencies they need to succeed in their roles, companies can reduce the likelihood of conflicts arising due to capability gaps or misunderstandings. Moreover, by fostering a culture of continuous learning and improvement within the channel network, organisations can create a shared sense of purpose and accountability, which can help prevent conflicts and drive long-term success.

Proactive conflict management is a critical component of effective channel management that requires a multifaceted approach encompassing clear expectations, open communication, collaborative problem-solving, data-driven insights, and partner development. By adopting a proactive and systematic approach to conflict management, companies can minimise the impact of disputes on channel performance, foster stronger and more productive partnerships, and drive long-term growth and success in an increasingly complex and competitive business landscape.

Challenges in Channel Management

Channel management is a complex and multifaceted endeavour that presents numerous challenges for organisations across industries. One of the primary challenges is achieving alignment and coordination among diverse channel partners, each with its own goals, priorities, and operating procedures. Ensuring seamless collaboration and communication across the distribution network requires significant effort and resources, as companies must navigate conflicting objectives, misaligned incentives, and varying levels of commitment from partners. Another major challenge is adapting to the rapid pace of technological change and evolving customer expectations. The rise of e-commerce, mobile commerce, and omnichannel retailing has disrupted traditional distribution models, forcing companies to rethink their channel strategies and invest in digital capabilities. Integrating online and offline channels while maintaining a consistent brand experience requires significant investments in technology, data analytics, and organisational transformation. Moreover, managing channel relationships in a globalised marketplace presents its own set of challenges, including cultural differences, regulatory complexities, and varying market dynamics across regions. Companies must navigate the intricacies of international trade, adapt their channel strategies to local market conditions, and build relationships with partners who possess the necessary local knowledge and expertise. The proliferation of data and the need for actionable insights also pose a challenge, as companies must develop robust data management systems and analytical tools to capture, integrate, and leverage vast amounts of information from various touchpoints along the distribution chain. Furthermore, maintaining channel control and mitigating risks associated with partner behaviour is an ongoing concern, as companies must strike a delicate balance between empowering partners and ensuring compliance with policies and standards.

To overcome these challenges, companies must adopt a proactive and strategic approach to channel management. This involves fostering open communication, building trust, and aligning incentives among partners to drive collaboration and minimise conflicts. Investing in digital technologies, such as CRM systems, PRM platforms, and data analytics tools, can enhance visibility, streamline processes, and enable data-driven decision-making. Developing a deep understanding of target markets, customer preferences, and local market dynamics is crucial for adapting channel strategies and selecting the right partners. Continuously monitoring market trends, competitive activities, and regulatory changes is essential for staying agile and responsive in the face of evolving challenges. By leveraging effective governance mechanisms, such as contracts, incentive structures, and monitoring systems, companies can align partner behaviour with business objectives and mitigate risks. Ultimately, navigating the challenges of channel management requires a combination of strategic vision.

CHAPTER 2

UNDERSTANDING CHANNEL DYNAMICS

Introduction to Channel Dynamics

Channel dynamics refers to the complex web of interactions and relationships that exist between the various actors involved in the distribution of products and services, from manufacturers to end consumers. These actors include manufacturers, wholesalers, retailers, distributors, and customers, each playing a unique role in the overall distribution process. The interplay between these entities creates a dynamic ecosystem that is constantly evolving, influenced by a myriad of factors such as market trends, technological advancements, changing consumer preferences, and competitive forces.

Understanding channel dynamics is crucial for businesses seeking to optimise their distribution strategies and achieve sustainable growth. By gaining insight into the intricacies of these relationships, companies can make informed decisions about how to structure their distribution networks, select the right partners, and adapt to changing market conditions. This knowledge also enables businesses to identify potential challenges and opportunities within their channels, such as power imbalances, conflicts of interest, or untapped market segments.

Moreover, a deep understanding of channel dynamics allows companies to develop more effective marketing and sales strategies. By knowing how products flow through the distribution chain, businesses can better target their promotional efforts, optimise pricing and packaging, and ensure that their products are available to the right customers at the right time and place. This insight also helps companies identify and address any bottlenecks or inefficiencies in their distribution processes, ultimately leading to improved customer satisfaction and loyalty.

In today's rapidly evolving business landscape, the importance of understanding channel dynamics cannot be overstated. With the rise of e-commerce, direct-to-consumer models, and omnichannel retailing, the traditional boundaries between manufacturers, wholesalers, and retailers are becoming increasingly blurred. This shift has created new opportunities for businesses to reach customers directly, bypass intermediaries, and create more personalised experiences. However, it has also introduced new challenges, such as increased competition, heightened customer expectations, and the need for seamless integration across multiple channels.

To navigate this complex landscape successfully, businesses must develop a holistic view of their distribution channels, taking into account the various actors, their roles, and the dynamic interactions between them. This requires a combination of strategic thinking, data-driven insights, and a willingness to adapt and innovate in response to changing market conditions. By embracing a customer-centric approach and fostering strong relationships with channel partners, companies can create a more agile, responsive, and resilient distribution network that can withstand the challenges of the modern business environment.

Introduction to Channel Dynamics (Continued)

Building upon the foundation established in the previous section, this chapter delves deeper into the complexities of channel dynamics and their impact on the overall performance of a company. It explores the various factors that shape the relationships between channel members, such as power structures, incentives, and communication flows, and how these dynamics can influence the effectiveness of a company's distribution strategy.

One of the key aspects of channel dynamics is the concept of channel conflict, which refers to the tensions and disagreements that can arise between different members of the distribution chain. These conflicts can stem from a variety of sources, such as competing goals, scarce resources, or misaligned incentives. For example, a manufacturer may want to maintain tight control over pricing and branding, while a retailer may prioritise maximising sales and profitability. If not managed effectively, these conflicts can lead to a breakdown in communication, a loss of trust, and, ultimately, a decline in channel performance.

To mitigate the risk of channel conflict and ensure the smooth functioning of the distribution network, companies must develop a clear understanding of the underlying drivers of these dynamics. This involves analysing the power relationships between channel members, identifying potential sources of tension, and developing strategies to align the interests of all parties involved. This may involve implementing incentive structures that reward collaboration and mutual success, establishing clear guidelines for communication and decision-making, and fostering a culture of transparency and trust.

Another critical aspect of channel dynamics is the role of information flow and data-sharing between channel members. In today's data-driven business environment, access to timely and accurate information is essential for making informed decisions and optimising channel performance. However, the sharing of sensitive data, such as customer information, sales figures, and inventory levels, can also create challenges and risks, particularly in terms of data privacy and security.

To address these challenges, companies must develop robust data governance frameworks and information-sharing protocols that balance the need for transparency and collaboration with the protection of confidential information. This may involve implementing secure data-sharing platforms, establishing clear data ownership and usage policies, and providing training and support to channel partners to ensure compliance with relevant regulations and best practices.

Furthermore, the chapter explores the impact of emerging technologies, such as artificial intelligence, the Internet of Things, and blockchain, on channel dynamics. These technologies have the potential to revolutionise the way products are distributed and sold by enabling real-time data exchange, automating processes, and creating new opportunities for personalisation and customisation. However, they also introduce new challenges, such as the need for significant investments in infrastructure and skills, the potential for disruption of existing business models, and the need for greater collaboration and standardisation across the distribution chain.

To harness the full potential of these technologies and navigate the challenges they present, companies must adopt a proactive and strategic approach to channel management. This involves staying up-to-date with the latest technological advancements, experimenting with new solutions and business models, and fostering a culture of innovation and continuous learning. By embracing a forward-looking perspective and collaborating closely with channel partners, companies can position themselves to thrive in the face of technological disruption and changing market dynamics.

Understanding channel dynamics is a critical component of effective distribution management in the modern business environment. By analysing the complex interplay of relationships, power structures, and information flows between channel members, companies can develop more effective strategies for mitigating conflicts, optimising performance, and driving growth. Moreover, by staying attuned to the impact of emerging technologies and adopting a proactive approach to channel management, businesses can position themselves to seize new opportunities and thrive in the face of change.

The Role of Channel Intermediaries

Channel intermediaries, such as wholesalers and distributors, play a crucial role in the distribution process by facilitating the flow of products and services from manufacturers to end consumers. These entities act as a bridge between producers and retailers, performing a range of essential functions that enable the smooth functioning of the distribution network.

One of the primary roles of channel intermediaries is to provide efficient distribution and logistics services. Wholesalers and distributors typically purchase products in bulk from manufacturers and then break them down into smaller quantities for distribution to retailers. This process allows manufacturers to focus on their core competencies of production and product development while leaving the complex tasks of inventory management, order processing, and shipping to specialised intermediaries.

By aggregating demand from multiple retailers and customers, channel intermediaries can achieve economies of scale in purchasing, warehousing, and transportation. This enables them to offer lower prices and better terms to their customers while also reducing the overall costs and complexity of the distribution process. Moreover, by maintaining large inventories and a broad network of relationships, intermediaries can help to ensure the availability of products and reduce the risk of stockouts or supply chain disruptions.

Another important function of channel intermediaries is to provide market intelligence and customer insights to manufacturers. As the direct link between producers and retailers, intermediaries are well-positioned to gather valuable information about market trends, customer preferences, and competitive dynamics. This data can help manufacturers refine their product offerings, adjust their pricing and promotional strategies, and identify new growth opportunities.

In addition, channel intermediaries can play a key role in providing value-added services to retailers and end customers. For example, wholesalers and distributors may offer product training and support, merchandising and display services, or even financing and credit options to help retailers manage their cash flow and inventory. By offering these services, intermediaries can help to differentiate themselves from competitors and build stronger relationships with their customers.

However, the role of channel intermediaries is not without its challenges and limitations. One potential drawback is the added cost and complexity that intermediaries can introduce into the distribution process. By acting as a middleman between manufacturers and retailers, intermediaries may add additional markups and fees that can erode profit margins and increase the final price to consumers.

Moreover, the presence of intermediaries can sometimes create a barrier between manufacturers and their end customers, limiting the ability of producers to gather direct feedback and insights about market trends and customer preferences. This can make it more difficult for manufacturers to develop targeted marketing and sales strategies and may limit their ability to respond quickly to changing market conditions.

To address these challenges, some manufacturers have chosen to bypass traditional intermediaries and establish direct-to-consumer (DTC) channels, such as e-commerce websites or branded retail stores. By selling directly to consumers, manufacturers can gain greater control over their distribution processes, gather more detailed customer data, and build stronger brand relationships. However, DTC strategies also come with their own set of challenges, such as the need for significant investments in logistics and fulfilment capabilities and the potential for channel conflict with existing retail partners.

Channel intermediaries play a vital role in the distribution process by providing efficient logistics services, market intelligence, and value-added support to manufacturers and retailers. While the presence of intermediaries can introduce additional costs and complexities into the distribution chain, they also offer significant benefits in terms of economies of scale, risk management, and customer service. As the business landscape continues to evolve, the role of channel intermediaries is likely to adapt and change, but their fundamental importance in facilitating the flow of products and services from producers to consumers is likely to remain constant.

The Role of Channel Intermediaries (Continued)

Building on the previous section, this page further explores the critical role that channel intermediaries play in bridging the gap between producers and customers. Beyond their essential functions in distribution and logistics, intermediaries also serve as valuable sources of market intelligence and customer insights, helping manufacturers to better understand and respond to the needs and preferences of their target audiences.

One of the key ways in which intermediaries provide market intelligence is through their close relationships with retailers and end customers. By interacting directly with these stakeholders on a regular basis, intermediaries gain a deep understanding of the factors that influence purchasing decisions, such as price sensitivity, product features, and brand preferences. They can also gather valuable feedback on the performance of specific products, as well as insights into emerging trends and competitive dynamics.

This information is invaluable to manufacturers, as it enables them to make more informed decisions about product development, pricing, and marketing strategies. By leveraging the insights provided by intermediaries, manufacturers can tailor their offerings to better meet the needs of their target customers, optimise their distribution channels, and stay ahead of the competition.

In addition to providing market intelligence, intermediaries also play a crucial role in facilitating communication and collaboration between different members of the distribution chain. As the central link between manufacturers and retailers, intermediaries are well-positioned to foster dialogue and build relationships between these parties, helping to ensure that everyone is working towards common goals and objectives.

For example, intermediaries may organise joint planning sessions or strategy meetings between manufacturers and retailers, where they can discuss upcoming product launches, promotional campaigns, and other key initiatives. They may also facilitate the sharing of data and insights between these parties, such as sales figures, inventory levels, and customer feedback, helping to create a more transparent and collaborative distribution network.

Furthermore, intermediaries can help resolve conflicts and disputes that may arise between different members of the distribution chain. By acting as a neutral third-party and leveraging their relationships and expertise, intermediaries can help to find mutually beneficial solutions to problems such as pricing disagreements, delivery delays, or quality control issues. This can help to maintain the smooth functioning of the distribution network and prevent minor issues from escalating into major disruptions.

However, it is important to note that the role of intermediaries in providing market intelligence and facilitating collaboration is not without its challenges. One potential issue is the risk of information asymmetry, where intermediaries may have access to more detailed or timely data than manufacturers or retailers. This can create an imbalance of power and make it difficult for all parties to make informed decisions and work together effectively.

To mitigate this risk, it is important for manufacturers and retailers to establish clear communication channels and data-sharing protocols with their intermediaries. This may involve setting up regular meetings or reports to discuss key metrics and insights, as well as establishing guidelines for the types of organisation can be shared and how it will be used. By fostering a culture of transparency and collaboration, all members of the distribution chain can work together more effectively to achieve their common goals.

Another challenge is the potential for intermediaries to prioritise their own interests over those of manufacturers or retailers. For example, an intermediary may be tempted to promote products that offer higher margins or sales commissions, even if they are not the best fit for a particular customer or market. To address this issue, manufacturers and retailers need to establish clear performance metrics and incentive structures that align the interests of all parties and encourage intermediaries to act in the best interests of the entire distribution network.

The role of channel intermediaries in providing market intelligence and facilitating collaboration is crucial for the success of any distribution network. By leveraging their unique position and expertise, intermediaries can help manufacturers and retailers to better understand and respond to the needs of their customers, optimise their operations, and work together more effectively. However, to fully realise these benefits, all members of the distribution chain need to establish clear communication channels, data-sharing protocols, and performance metrics that foster transparency, collaboration, and alignment of interests.

Channel Power and Influence

Channel power and influence refer to the ability of different members of the distribution chain to exert control over the flow of products, information, and financial resources. Understanding the dynamics of power and influence within a distribution network is crucial for manufacturers, as it can have a significant impact on their ability to achieve their strategic objectives and maintain a competitive advantage.

One of the primary sources of channel power is the control over critical resources, such as raw materials, production facilities, or intellectual property. Manufacturers that possess unique or proprietary technologies, for example, may have significant leverage over their channel partners, as they can dictate the terms of production, pricing, and distribution. Similarly, manufacturers with strong brand recognition and customer loyalty may have greater bargaining power when negotiating with retailers or distributors, as their products are in high demand and can drive sales and profitability.

Another important factor that can influence channel power is the size and scale of the different members of the distribution chain. Large retailers or distributors, for example, may have significant buying power and can negotiate more favourable terms with manufacturers, such as lower prices, longer payment terms, or exclusive distribution rights. This can put smaller manufacturers at a disadvantage, as they may struggle to compete with the economies of scale and market reach of their larger counterparts.

In addition to these structural factors, channel power can also be influenced by the relationships and alliances between different members of the distribution chain. Manufacturers that have strong, long-standing relationships with key retailers or distributors may have greater influence and bargaining power, as they can leverage these partnerships to secure more favourable terms and support. Similarly, manufacturers that are able to form strategic alliances or joint ventures with other members of the distribution chain may be able to pool their resources and expertise to achieve greater market power and competitiveness.

However, it is important to note that channel power is not a static or absolute concept but rather a dynamic and relative one. The balance of power within a distribution network can shift over time as market conditions, customer preferences, and competitive dynamics evolve. Manufacturers that are able to anticipate and adapt to these changes and that are able to leverage their unique strengths and capabilities will be better positioned to maintain their channel power and influence over the long-term.

To effectively manage channel power and influence, manufacturers need to take a strategic and proactive approach to their relationships with channel partners. This may involve developing a deep understanding of the needs and motivations of different members of the distribution chain and tailoring their value propositions and incentives accordingly. It may also involve investing in long-term partnerships and alliances and working collaboratively with channel partners to identify and pursue new growth opportunities.

Another key aspect of managing channel power and influence is the ability to effectively negotiate and resolve conflicts with channel partners. Manufacturers who are able to maintain open and transparent communication with their partners and who are willing to find mutually beneficial solutions to disputes or disagreements will be better positioned to maintain their channel power and influence over time.

The key to success in managing channel power and influence is to take a holistic and strategic approach that considers the needs and motivations of all members of the distribution chain. By fostering strong, collaborative relationships with channel partners and by leveraging their unique strengths and capabilities, manufacturers can create a more balanced and effective distribution network that delivers value to all stakeholders.

Channel Power and Influence (Continued)

As businesses navigate the complex landscape of channel power and influence, they must be equipped with a deep understanding of the sources and dynamics that shape these forces. This knowledge is essential for developing effective strategies to manage relationships, resolve conflicts, and drive mutually beneficial outcomes within the distribution network.

One of the key challenges in managing channel power and influence is the inherent tension between cooperation and competition among channel members. While all parties in the distribution chain share a common goal of delivering value to end customers, they also have their own individual objectives and priorities. Manufacturers, for example, may be focused on maximising production efficiency and maintaining brand integrity, while retailers may be more concerned with optimising shelf space and driving sales volume.

To navigate these competing interests and foster collaborative relationships, companies must be skilled in the art of negotiation and conflict resolution. This requires a keen understanding of the underlying motivations and pain points of each channel member, as well as the ability to find creative solutions that balance the needs of all parties involved. Effective negotiation strategies may include techniques such as active listening, empathy, and the use of objective criteria to evaluate options and arrive at fair outcomes.

Another important aspect of managing channel power and influence is the ability to leverage data and analytics to inform decision-making and strategy development. In today's digital age, businesses have access to a wealth of information about customer behaviour, market trends, and competitive dynamics. By harnessing the power of this data, companies can gain deeper insights into the factors that drive channel performance and identify opportunities for improvement.

For example, manufacturers can use point-of-sale data from retailers to track product performance, identify top-selling SKUs, and optimise inventory levels. They can also leverage customer feedback and reviews to inform product development and marketing strategies and to identify areas where they may need to provide additional support or training to channel partners.

Similarly, retailers can use data analytics to optimise their assortment planning, pricing strategies, and promotional activities. By understanding which products are most popular with customers and which ones drive the highest margins, retailers can make more informed decisions about which items to stock and how to allocate shelf space.

Channel Structure and Design

Channel structure and design play a crucial role in determining the effectiveness and efficiency of a distribution network. The way in which products and services flow from manufacturers to end customers can have a significant impact on factors such as cost, speed, flexibility, and customer satisfaction.

One of the key decisions in channel design is the choice between direct and indirect distribution models. In a direct distribution model, manufacturers sell their products directly to end customers, without the use of intermediaries such as wholesalers or retailers. This approach can provide greater control over the customer experience, as well as higher margins, as manufacturers are able to capture the full value of each sale.

However, direct distribution also comes with its own challenges and limitations. For example, manufacturers may need to invest heavily in their own sales and distribution capabilities, including logistics, customer service, and marketing. They may also struggle to achieve the same level of market coverage and scale as indirect distribution models, particularly in larger or more fragmented markets.

Indirect distribution, on the other hand, involves the use of intermediaries to help bring products to market. This can take many forms, such as selling through wholesalers, distributors, or retailers, each of which can offer different benefits and trade-offs. For example, selling through wholesalers can provide access to a larger customer base and more efficient logistics, while selling through retailers can offer greater control over the in-store experience and customer relationships.

Another important consideration in channel design is the degree of vertical integration between different members of the distribution chain. Vertical integration refers to the extent to which a company owns or controls the different stages of the value chain, from raw materials to finished products. In a highly vertically integrated model, a manufacturer may own and operate its own production facilities, distribution centres, and retail stores, giving it complete control over the entire process.

However, vertical integration can also be costly and inflexible, as it requires significant capital investments and can limit a company's ability to adapt to changing market conditions. In contrast, a more vertically disintegrated model, in which different members of the distribution chain operate independently, can provide greater flexibility and specialisation but may also create challenges in terms of coordination and alignment.

The optimal channel structure and design will depend on a variety of factors, including the nature of the products being sold, the characteristics of the target market, the competitive landscape, and the company's own capabilities and resources. By carefully considering these factors and weighing the trade-offs between different options, companies can develop a channel strategy that maximises their chances of success and delivers value to all stakeholders.

Channel Structure and Design (Continued)

In addition to the high-level decisions around direct vs. indirect distribution and vertical integration, there are many other important considerations in channel structure and design. One key factor is the degree of channel intensity, which refers to the number and type of intermediaries used to bring products to market.

In an intensive distribution strategy, a company may seek to make its products available through as many outlets as possible in order to maximise market coverage and sales volume. This approach is often used for products with broad appeal and low unit costs, such as consumer packaged goods or fast-moving consumer electronics.

However, intensive distribution can also create challenges in terms of channel management and control. With a large number of intermediaries involved, it can be difficult to ensure consistent pricing, promotion, and customer experience across all touchpoints. This can lead to channel conflict, where different members of the distribution chain may compete against each other for sales and margins.

In contrast, a selective or exclusive distribution strategy involves limiting the number of intermediaries that are authorised to sell a company's products. This approach can provide greater control over the brand experience and help to maintain a premium positioning in the market. It can also help to build stronger relationships with key channel partners, as they are given a larger share of the business and more support from the manufacturer.

However, selective, or exclusive distribution may also limit a company's ability to reach certain customer segments or geographic markets and may require more investment in sales and marketing support for each individual channel partner.

Another important consideration in channel design is the use of multi-channel or omnichannel strategies, which involve selling products through multiple types of intermediaries and touchpoints. For example, a company may sell its products through a combination of owned e-commerce websites, third-party marketplaces, brick-and-mortar retail stores, and mobile apps.

Multi-channel strategies can provide customers with greater choice and convenience and can help companies reach different customer segments and market opportunities. However, they can also create challenges in terms of data integration, inventory management, and customer experience consistency across different channels.

To address these challenges, many companies are adopting an omnichannel approach, which seeks to provide a seamless and integrated customer experience across all touchpoints. This involves breaking down silos between different channels and departments and using data and technology to create a unified view of the customer and their interactions with the brand.

The key to successful channel structure and design is to strike the right balance between reach, control, and customer experience. By carefully considering the trade-offs between different options and adapting to changing market conditions and customer needs, companies can develop a channel strategy that maximises their chances of success and delivers value to all stakeholders over the long-term.

Channel Evolution and Change

The world of business is constantly evolving, and nowhere is this more evident than in the realm of distribution channels. As customer preferences, technological advancements, and market forces continue to reshape the way products and services are delivered, companies must remain vigilant and adaptable to stay ahead of the curve. The ability to anticipate and respond to change has become a critical success factor in today's fast-paced and highly competitive business environment.

One of the most significant drivers of channel evolution in recent years has been the rapid growth of e-commerce and digital platforms. The rise of online shopping has fundamentally transformed the retail landscape, as customers increasingly expect the convenience, choice, and personalisation that digital channels can provide. This shift has created new opportunities for manufacturers and retailers alike, as they can now reach customers directly through their own websites and mobile apps, bypassing traditional intermediaries and reducing costs.

However, the growth of e-commerce has also created new challenges and risks for companies, particularly in terms of channel conflict and cannibalisation. As manufacturers and retailers compete for online sales and customer loyalty, they may inadvertently undermine their relationships with traditional channel partners, leading to tensions and disputes. Moreover, the ease of price comparison and the proliferation of third-party marketplaces can put downward pressure on margins and make it harder for companies to maintain a premium positioning in the market.

To address these challenges, many companies are adopting a more holistic and integrated approach to channel management, one that seeks to balance the benefits and risks of different channels and create a seamless customer experience across all touchpoints. This may involve developing a clear and consistent brand strategy, investing in data analytics and customer insights, and fostering closer collaboration and communication with channel partners.

Another important trend in channel evolution is the growing importance of sustainability and social responsibility in the distribution chain. As consumers become more aware of the environmental and social impact of their purchasing decisions, they are increasingly seeking out products and brands that align with their values and beliefs. This has created new opportunities for companies to differentiate themselves based on their commitment to sustainability, ethical sourcing, and community engagement.

However, the pursuit of sustainability and social responsibility in the distribution chain also comes with its own challenges and trade-offs. For example, sourcing materials and products from more sustainable or ethical suppliers may increase costs and lead times, while implementing more environmentally friendly packaging and logistics may require significant investments in new technologies and processes.

To navigate these challenges and seize the opportunities of sustainability and social responsibility, companies must take a strategic and long-term view of their distribution networks. This may involve developing closer partnerships with suppliers and other stakeholders, investing in new technologies and innovations, and communicating their commitments and progress to customers and other stakeholders in a transparent and authentic way.

The key to success in the face of channel evolution and change is to remain agile, adaptable, and customer-centric. By staying attuned to changing market conditions and customer needs, investing in new capabilities and technologies, and fostering a culture of innovation and experimentation, companies can position themselves to thrive in the face of disruption and uncertainty. As the famous quote goes, "The only constant in life is change," and those who embrace it with courage and creativity will be the ones who shape the future of their industries.

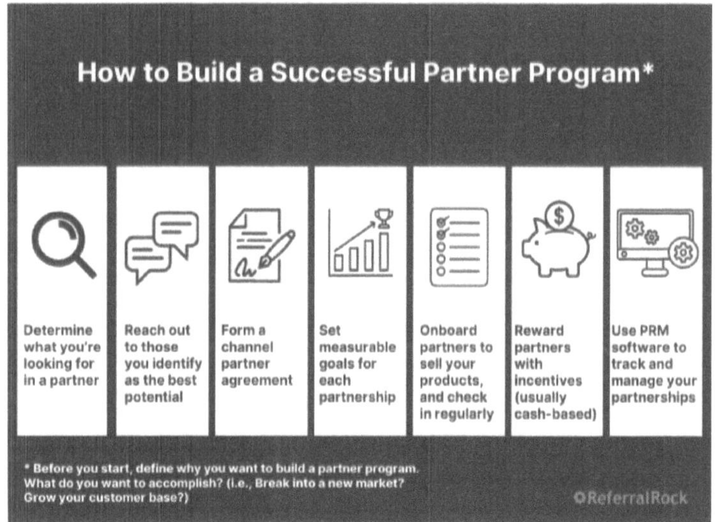

CHAPTER 3

DEVELOPING A CHANNEL PARTNER PROGRAMME

Introduction

This introduction highlights the critical role that channel partners play in driving business growth and market expansion. It will emphasise how leveraging channel partners can help companies reach new customers, enter new markets, and scale their operations more efficiently. The purpose and objectives of the chapter will be clearly outlined, setting the stage for the comprehensive discussion of developing a successful channel partner programme.

I. Aligning Channel Partner Programme with Business Strategy

This section will delve into the importance of aligning the channel partner programme with the overall business strategy. It will guide readers on how to define clear goals and objectives for the programme, ensuring that they are in sync with the company's overarching mission and vision. The section will also discuss the significance of identifying target markets and customer segments and how channel partners can be strategically leveraged to reach these desired audiences. By determining the specific role that channel partners will play in achieving business objectives, companies can create a focused and effective programme.

II. Identifying the Right Channel Partners

Selecting the right channel partners is a critical step in building a successful programme. This section will provide a detailed guide on conducting thorough market research and competitive analysis to identify potential partners. It will discuss the development of partner selection criteria, taking into account factors such as industry expertise, market reach, resources, and reputation. The section will also delve into the process of profiling ideal partners based on their capabilities and alignment with the company's values and culture. By carefully evaluating and selecting partners, companies can ensure a strong foundation for their channel partner programme.

III. Building Strong Relationships with Channel Partners

Strong relationships are the cornerstone of successful channel partnerships. This section will explore the key elements of building and nurturing these relationships. It will discuss the importance of establishing effective communication channels, including regular meetings, updates, and feedback mechanisms. The section will also highlight the role of fostering collaboration and trust through transparent and open dialogue. Providing comprehensive training, support, and sales enablement resources will be emphasised as critical factors in empowering partners to succeed. Additionally, the section will discuss the significance of recognising and rewarding partner achievements to maintain motivation and loyalty.

IV. Creating a Structured Channel Partner Programme

A well-structured channel partner programme is essential for setting clear expectations and driving partner performance. This section will guide readers through the process of developing a robust programme framework. It will discuss the importance of defining partner expectations, benefits, and requirements upfront, creating a clear understanding of the partnership dynamics. The section will also explore the establishment of training and certification processes to ensure partners have the necessary knowledge and skills to effectively represent the company's products or services. Implementing incentive and reward programmes will be highlighted as key motivators for partner performance. Additionally, the section will discuss the value of providing marketing support and co-branding opportunities to enhance partner visibility and credibility in the market.

V. Differentiating and Tailoring Programmes for Partner Types

Recognising that not all partners are the same, this section will emphasise the importance of differentiating and tailoring channel partner programmes based on partner types and tiers. It will guide readers on how to identify different partner categories based on their capabilities, market focus, and strategic value to the company. The section will discuss the process of customising programme elements, such as training, support, and incentives, to align with the specific needs and expectations of each partner type. Creating a compelling partner value proposition will be highlighted as a crucial aspect of attracting and retaining partners. The section will also discuss the importance of maintaining programme flexibility to accommodate the diverse requirements of different partners.

VI. Engaging in Regular Communication and Collaboration

Effective communication and collaboration are essential for maintaining strong and productive channel partnerships. This section will provide strategies for engaging partners through regular updates, meetings, and joint planning sessions. It will discuss the importance of soliciting partner feedback and insights to gain valuable market intelligence and identify areas for improvement. The section will also highlight the significance of addressing partner concerns and challenges promptly to maintain trust and loyalty. Celebrating joint successes and milestones will be emphasised as a way to strengthen the partnership bond and keep partners motivated.

VII. Leveraging Technology for Partner Enablement

Technology plays a crucial role in streamlining and optimising channel partner operations. This section will explore how companies can leverage various technological tools to enable and support their partners. It will discuss the implementation of partner relationship management (PRM) systems to centralise partner information, track interactions, and automate key processes. The section will also highlight the value of providing self-service partner portals and resources, allowing partners to access relevant information and tools at their convenience. Automating processes, such as lead distribution, deal registration, and performance tracking, will be discussed as ways to improve efficiency, and reduce administrative burden on partners. Additionally, the section will explore the use of data analytics to gain insights into partner performance and identify opportunities for optimisation.

VIII. Monitoring and Measuring Channel Partner Performance

Measuring and monitoring channel partner performance is critical for ensuring the effectiveness and ROI of the programme. This section will guide readers on defining key performance indicators (KPIs) that align with the programme's goals and objectives. It will discuss the process of setting realistic performance targets and benchmarks for partners to strive towards. The section will also explore the use of data analytics and reporting tools to track partner performance across various metrics, such as sales revenue, customer acquisition, and engagement levels. Conducting regular performance reviews and assessments will be highlighted as a way to provide feedback, identify areas for improvement, and make data-driven decisions. The section will also discuss the importance of providing coaching and support to help partners improve their performance and achieve their targets.

IX. Continuously Improving the Channel Partner Programme

A successful channel partner programme requires continuous evaluation and improvement to stay relevant and effective in a dynamic market landscape. This section will discuss the importance of gathering partner feedback through various methods, such as surveys, focus groups, and advisory councils. It will guide readers in analysing programme effectiveness by assessing key metrics, partner satisfaction levels, and market impact. The section will also explore the process of identifying areas for improvement based on partner input, market trends, and best practices. Implementing programme enhancements and communicating changes to partners will be highlighted as critical steps in keeping the programme up-to-date and valuable. Additionally, the section will discuss the importance of monitoring industry developments and adapting the programme accordingly to maintain a competitive education

X. Ensuring Financial Viability and ROI

Financial viability and return on investment (ROI) are crucial considerations for any channel partner programme. This section will guide readers on modelling programme economics and creating financial projections to assess the programme's potential impact on revenue and profitability. It will discuss the process of defining partner compensation and incentive structures that align with the company's financial goals while providing sufficient motivation for partners. The section will also highlight the importance of monitoring programme costs and ROI regularly to ensure the programme remains financially sustainable. Strategies for adjusting programme elements, such as pricing, margins, and incentives, will be explored as ways to optimise financial performance and maintain a healthy bottom line.

XI. Securing Internal Organisational Alignment and Support

Developing a successful channel partner programme requires the alignment and support of various internal stakeholders across the organisation. This section will discuss the importance of engaging key stakeholders from different departments, such as sales, marketing, product development, and customer service, in the programme's planning and execution. It will guide readers on communicating the programme's value and benefits to internal teams, highlighting how channel partners can contribute to overall business success. The section will also explore strategies for aligning incentives and goals across the organisation to ensure everyone is working towards common objectives. Providing internal training and resources on channel partner engagement will be emphasised as a way to build a culture of collaboration and support for the programme.

Conclusion

The conclusion will summarise the key elements and best practices discussed throughout the chapter, reinforcing the importance of developing a strategic, structured, and partner-centric channel programme. It will reiterate the value of continuous evaluation and improvement to ensure the programme remains relevant and effective in driving business growth. The conclusion will also emphasise the significance of adapting to market changes and evolving partner needs to maintain a competitive edge. Finally, it will include a call to action, encouraging readers to assess their current channel partner strategies and take proactive steps to implement or enhance their programmes based on the insights and recommendations provided in the chapter.

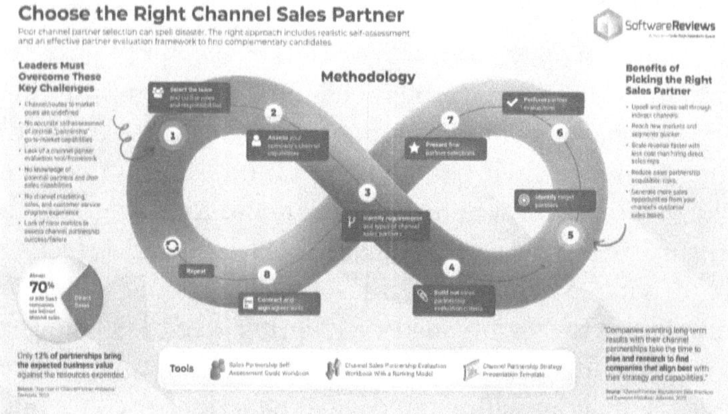

CHAPTER 4

PARTNER SELECTION AND RECRUITMENT

In the complex ecosystem of channel management, the selection and recruitment of the right partners stand as critical pillars of success. The choice of channel partners can significantly influence a company's ability to effectively reach target markets, drive sales, and deliver value to customers. This chapter delves into the importance of partner selection, explores strategies for partner recruitment, outlines key considerations when evaluating potential channel partners, and discusses best practices for onboarding and training these partners to ensure a successful and mutually beneficial relationship.

The selection of channel partners is a strategic decision that can have far-reaching implications for a company's performance and market presence. The right partners can provide access to new markets, enhance brand visibility, and contribute to the overall success of the company's channel strategy (Gilliland, 2003). Partners bring valuable resources, expertise, and relationships to the table, enabling companies to expand their reach and tap into new customer segments (Cavusgil et al., 2004). They can also help companies overcome barriers to entry, such as cultural differences, regulatory challenges, and local market dynamics (Samiee et al., 2015).

However, selecting the wrong partners can have detrimental effects on a company's channel strategy. Misaligned goals, incompatible cultures, and conflicting priorities can lead to channel conflicts, erode trust, and damage the company's reputation (Mehta et al., 2000). Poor partner performance, whether due to lack of capabilities or commitment, can hinder the company's ability to meet customer needs and achieve its sales targets (Jap & Ganesan, 2000). Therefore, it is crucial for companies to approach partner selection with utmost care and diligence.

Effective partner selection requires a clear understanding of the company's channel strategy, target markets, and value proposition. Companies must define the ideal partner profile, considering factors such as market coverage, industry expertise, financial stability, and cultural fit (Geigenmüller & Bettis-Outland, 2012). They should also establish specific criteria and metrics to evaluate potential partners objectively and consistently (Brouthers et al., 2008).

One key consideration in partner selection is the alignment of goals and values. Partners should share the company's vision, objectives, and commitment to delivering superior customer value (Mehta et al., 2006). They should also demonstrate a willingness to invest in the partnership, whether through dedicated resources, joint marketing efforts, or technology adoption (Srinivasan et al., 2011). Alignment ensures that partners are motivated to work towards common goals and can collaborate effectively to overcome challenges and seize opportunities.

Another critical factor is the partner's market knowledge and customer relationships. Partners should have a deep understanding of the local market dynamics, customer preferences, and competitive landscape (Homburg et al., 2002). They should also have established relationships with key customers, influencers, and decision-makers in the target market (Palmatier et al., 2007). This market intelligence and customer access can help companies tailor their offerings, marketing messages, and sales strategies to meet specific market needs and drive customer adoption.

In addition to market knowledge, partners should possess the necessary capabilities and resources to effectively sell and support the company's products or services. This includes having the right sales and technical skills, as well as the infrastructure and processes to manage customer interactions, handle orders, and provide after-sales support (Frazier & Summers, 1984). Partners should also have the financial stability and scalability to invest in growth and adapt to changing market conditions (Jap & Ganesan, 2000).

Once the ideal partner profile is defined, companies can employ various strategies for partner recruitment. One approach is to leverage existing networks and relationships, such as current customers, suppliers, or industry associations, to identify potential partners with proven track records and relevant expertise (Gençtürk & Aulakh, 2007). Referrals from trusted sources can provide valuable insights into a potential partner's reputation, capabilities, and performance history.

Another strategy is to proactively seek out and engage with potential partners through targeted outreach and marketing efforts. This can involve attending industry events, participating in trade shows, and leveraging digital channels such as social media and online partner portals to connect with prospective partners (Saini et al., 2010). By communicating the value proposition and benefits of the partnership, companies can attract high-quality partners that share their vision and goals.

Once potential partners are identified, a rigorous evaluation process should be conducted to assess their suitability and fit. This evaluation should encompass multiple dimensions, including the partner's market presence, financial stability, technical capabilities, and cultural compatibility (Brouthers et al., 2008). Companies should also assess the partner's ability to meet performance expectations, such as sales targets, customer satisfaction levels, and compliance with company policies and standards (Gilliland, 2003).

After selecting the right partners, the focus shifts to onboarding and training them effectively. Onboarding involves familiarising partners with the company's products, processes, and expectations and ensuring a smooth integration into the channel ecosystem (Frazier & Summers, 1984). Training programmes should cover both technical and sales-related topics, equipping partners with the knowledge and skills necessary to represent the company's brand and sell its offerings successfully (Kotler et al., 2013).

Ongoing support, communication, and performance management are critical for fostering long-term, mutually beneficial relationships with channel partners. Regular feedback, performance reviews, and joint planning sessions can help align goals, address challenges, and identify opportunities for improvement and growth (Anderson & Weitz, 1992). By providing partners with the tools, resources, and incentives to succeed, companies can build strong, committed partnerships that drive business success.

Partner selection and recruitment are essential components of effective channel management. By carefully selecting partners that align with the company's goals, values, and target markets and by providing comprehensive onboarding, training, and support, companies can build a robust and high-performing channel network. Investing time and resources in finding the right partners and nurturing those relationships can lead to increased market coverage, sales growth, and competitive advantage in the long run.

Importance of Partner Selection

The selection of channel partners is indeed a strategic decision with significant implications for a company's performance and market presence. Gilliland (2003) highlights how the right partners can provide access to new markets, enhance brand visibility, and contribute to the overall success of the company's channel strategy. Partners bring valuable resources, expertise, and relationships to the table, enabling companies to expand their reach and tap into new customer segments (Cavusgil et al., 2004). They can also help companies overcome barriers to entry, such as cultural differences, regulatory challenges, and local market dynamics (Samiee et al., 2015).

On the other hand, Mehta et al. (2000) warn that partnering with the wrong entities can lead to misaligned goals, channel conflicts, and erosion of brand reputation. Poor partner selection can result in partners who lack the necessary capabilities, commitment, or cultural fit to effectively represent the company's brand and meet customer needs. This can lead to subpar performance, damaged relationships, and, ultimately, a weakened market position (Jap & Ganesan, 2000). Therefore, effective partner selection is crucial for leveraging the strengths, market knowledge, and customer relationships of channel partners. Cavusgil et al. (2004) emphasise the importance of carefully choosing partners that align with the company's values, target customer segments, and strategic objectives. This alignment enables organisations to enhance their competitive advantage and drive sustainable growth. By selecting partners with complementary capabilities and resources, companies can create synergies that foster innovation, efficiency, and value creation within the channel ecosystem (Sarkar et al., 2001).

To ensure successful partner selection, companies must define clear criteria and processes for evaluating potential partners. This includes assessing factors such as market coverage, industry expertise, financial stability, and cultural fit (Geigenmüller & Bettis-Outland, 2012). By establishing a structured approach to partner selection, companies can make informed decisions and minimise the risks associated with partnering with the wrong entities.

Moreover, ongoing management and support of channel partnerships are critical for maintaining alignment and driving long-term success. Regular communication, performance monitoring, and joint problem-solving can help identify and address any issues that may arise, such as goal misalignment or conflict (Anderson & Weitz, 1992). By investing in the development and nurturing of channel partnerships, companies can build trust, commitment, and a shared vision for growth (Mohr & Spekman, 1994). In summary, the selection of channel partners is a strategic decision that can significantly impact a company's performance and market presence. The right partners can provide valuable resources, expertise, and access to new markets, while the wrong partners can lead to misaligned goals, conflicts, and damage to the brand. Effective partner selection involves carefully choosing partners that align with the company's values, target segments, and objectives and leveraging their complementary capabilities to drive innovation and growth. By establishing clear selection criteria, ongoing management, and support, companies can build successful and mutually beneficial channel partnerships.

Strategies for Partner Recruitment

Recruiting the right channel partners is indeed a critical task that requires a well-defined and proactive approach. As Geigenmüller and Bettis-Outland (2012) suggest, companies must develop a clear understanding of their ideal partner profile, considering factors such as market coverage, industry expertise, financial stability, and cultural fit. This helps in establishing specific criteria and guidelines for partner selection, which can streamline the recruitment process and ensure consistency in the partner network.

One effective strategy for partner recruitment, as mentioned, is leveraging existing networks and relationships. Gençtürk and Aulakh (2007) highlight the value of tapping into current customer base, suppliers, and industry associations to identify potential partners with proven track records and relevant expertise. Referrals from trusted sources can provide valuable insights into a potential partner's reputation, capabilities, and performance history, helping companies make informed decisions about partner selection.

For example, a company in the IT industry looking to expand its channel network could reach out to its existing enterprise customers and ask for referrals of reliable distributors or resellers they have worked with. The company could also engage with industry associations or attend trade shows specific to their target market to network with potential partners who have demonstrated expertise and success in that domain.

Another approach to partner recruitment is actively seeking out and engaging with potential partners through targeted outreach and marketing efforts. Saini et al.

(2010) suggest attending industry events, participating in trade shows, and leveraging digital channels such as social media and online partner portals to connect with prospective partners. By proactively communicating the value proposition and benefits of the partnership, companies can attract high-quality partners that share their vision and goals.

For instance, a customer goods company looking to expand into new geographic markets could identify potential distributors in those regions and reach out to them with a compelling partnership proposal. The company could highlight its brand reputation, product quality, marketing support, and growth potential to attract partners who are well-positioned to help them succeed in those markets.

In addition to these strategies, companies can also consider creating a formal partner recruitment programme with clearly defined benefits, requirements, and processes. This can help attract partners who are serious about the opportunity and willing to invest in the relationship. The programme could include elements such as a partner portal with resources and training materials, a tiered incentive structure based on performance, and dedicated partner support teams.

Overall, effective partner recruitment requires a combination of leveraging existing relationships, proactive outreach, and a well-structured partner programme. By defining the ideal partner profile, establishing clear selection criteria, and communicating the value of the partnership, companies can attract the right partners to help them achieve their channel goals.

Here are a few more examples of partner recruitment strategies:

1. **Referral incentives:** Companies can offer incentives to their existing partners or customers for referring new partners who meet the specified criteria. This can help tap into the networks of trusted sources and encourage them to actively seek out potential partners on the company's behalf.

2. **Online partner recruitment:** Companies can create a dedicated partner recruitment page on their website, outlining the benefits of partnering, the requirements for becoming a partner, and a form for interested parties to apply. This can help attract partners who are actively searching for opportunities and make it easy for them to express interest.

3. **Targeted advertising:** Companies can use targeted advertising on social media, industry publications, or search engines to reach potential partners who fit their ideal profile. The ads could highlight the key benefits of partnering and direct interested parties to a landing page with more information and an application form.

4. **Partner recruitment events:** Companies can host exclusive events for potential partners, such as webinars, roundtables, or networking dinners, to showcase their offerings, share success stories, and build relationships with prospective partners. These events can help create a sense of exclusivity and value for the partnership opportunity.

5. **Channel partner marketplace:** Companies can explore online channel partner marketplaces, such as PartnerStack or PartnerPort, which connect vendors with potential partners based on specific criteria and preferences. These platforms can help streamline the partner recruitment process and provide access to a larger pool of qualified candidates.

By employing a mix of these strategies and tailoring them to their specific industry and target market, companies can effectively recruit the right channel partners to support their growth and success.

Evaluating Potential Channel Partners

Once potential channel partners have been identified, it is indeed crucial to conduct a thorough evaluation to assess their suitability and fit within the company's channel strategy. As Brouthers et al. (2008) suggest, this evaluation process should encompass multiple dimensions, including the partner's market presence, financial stability, technical capabilities, and cultural compatibility. By considering these factors, companies can make informed decisions about which partners are best positioned to help them achieve their channel goals.

One key consideration when evaluating potential partners is their ability to effectively serve the target customer segments. Homburg et al. (2002) emphasise the importance of partners having a deep understanding of customer needs, preferences, and buying behaviours within the specific markets they operate in. This local market knowledge is essential for partners to effectively promote and sell the company's products or services to the right customers through the right channels.

For example, a company selling high-end customer electronics may evaluate potential partners based on their experience and success in serving affluent, tech-savvy customers in specific geographic regions. The company would want to ensure that the partner has the necessary sales and marketing capabilities to effectively reach and engage this target segment, such as a knowledgeable sales staff, attractive retail locations, and targeted marketing campaigns.

Another important factor to assess is the partner's alignment with the company's values and strategic objectives. As Mehta et al. (2006) point out, partners should demonstrate a shared commitment to quality, customer satisfaction, and long-term success. Evaluating the partner's track record, reputation, and references from previous collaborations can provide valuable insights into their business practices and reliability.

For instance, a company with a strong emphasis on sustainability and corporate social responsibility may evaluate potential partners based on their environmental practices, ethical sourcing, and community involvement. The company would want to ensure that the partner's values and actions align with their own to maintain brand consistency and avoid reputational risks.

Financial stability and viability are also critical considerations when evaluating potential partners. As Jap and Ganesan (2000) suggest, companies should assess the partner's financial health, credit history, and ability to invest in the necessary resources and infrastructure to support the partnership. Partners with a strong financial foundation are more likely to have the capacity to scale operations, adapt to market changes, and fulfil their commitments within the channel relationship.

For example, a company looking to expand into new markets may evaluate potential partners based on their financial stability, growth potential, and willingness to invest in joint marketing and sales efforts. The company would want to ensure that the partner has the necessary resources and motivation to support the expansion strategy and grow the business together over the long-term.

In addition to these factors, companies should also consider the partner's technical capabilities and infrastructure. This is particularly important for products or services that require specialised knowledge, skills, or equipment to sell and support effectively. Partners should have the necessary technical expertise, training programmes, and support systems in place to ensure customer satisfaction and minimise operational risks.

Finally, cultural compatibility is another critical factor to consider when evaluating potential partners. As Mehta et al. (2006) suggest, cultural differences can impact communication, decision-making, and conflict resolution within the channel relationship. Companies should assess the partner's organisational culture, values, and communication style to ensure a good fit with their own culture and ways of working.

For instance, a company with a highly collaborative and transparent culture may evaluate potential partners based on their willingness to share information, engage in joint planning, and work together to solve problems. The company would want to ensure that the partner's culture supports open communication, trust, and mutual respect to foster a strong and productive partnership.

Overall, evaluating potential channel partners requires a comprehensive and multidimensional approach. By considering factors such as market knowledge, strategic alignment, financial stability, technical capabilities, and cultural compatibility, companies can select partners who are well-positioned to help them achieve their channel goals and grow their business together over the long-term.

Here are a few more examples of how companies can evaluate potential channel partners:

1. **Partner profile scorecard:** Companies can create a scorecard with weighted criteria based on their ideal partner profile, such as market coverage, sales performance, technical expertise, and customer satisfaction ratings. Potential partners can be evaluated against these criteria to determine their overall fit and potential value to the company.

2. **On-site visits and assessments:** Companies can conduct on-site visits to potential partners' facilities, offices, or retail locations to assess their operations, infrastructure, and customer engagement firsthand. This can provide valuable insights into the partner's capabilities, processes, and culture that may not be apparent through remote evaluations.

3. **Customer references and case studies:** Companies can ask potential partners to provide references from their existing customers or share case studies of successful projects or implementations. This can help validate the partner's track record, industry expertise, and ability to deliver value to customers in similar markets or segments.

4. **Partner business plan and financial projections:** Companies can request potential partners to submit a business plan outlining their go-to-market strategy, sales and marketing plans, and financial projections for the partnership. This can help assess the partner's level of commitment, strategic thinking, and financial viability over the long-term.

5. **Cultural fit assessment**: Companies can use cultural fit assessment tools, such as surveys or interviews, to evaluate potential partners' organisational culture, values, and communication style. This can help identify potential cultural gaps or misalignments early on and ensure a smoother partnership down the road.

By using a combination of these evaluation methods and criteria, companies can gain a comprehensive understanding of potential partners' strengths, weaknesses, and overall fit with their channel strategy. This can help them make more informed and data-driven decisions about which partners to recruit and invest in for long-term success.

Onboarding and Training Channel Partners

Once the right channel partners have been selected, the focus shifts to effectively onboarding and training them to ensure a smooth integration into the company's channel ecosystem. Onboarding involves familiarising partners with the company's products, services, processes, and expectations (Frazier & Summers, 1984). This process should be comprehensive, covering aspects such as product features, pricing structures, marketing guidelines, and technical support.

Training channel partners is essential to equip them with the knowledge and skills necessary to effectively represent the company's brand and sell its offerings. Training programmes should cover both technical and sales-related topics, including product specifications, competitive positioning, customer engagement strategies, and closing techniques (Kotler et al., 2013). By investing in robust training initiatives, companies can ensure that their partners have the expertise and confidence to drive sales and deliver exceptional customer experiences.

Moreover, ongoing support and communication are crucial for maintaining strong relationships with channel partners. Regular updates, performance reviews, and feedback sessions can help identify areas for improvement, address challenges, and foster a culture of continuous learning and growth (Anderson & Weitz, 1992). By providing partners with the tools, resources, and support they need to succeed, companies can build long-term, mutually beneficial partnerships that drive business success.

In conclusion, partner selection and recruitment are critical components of effective channel management.

By carefully selecting partners that align with the company's values, goals, and target markets, organisations can build a strong and competitive channel network. Evaluating potential partners based on multiple criteria, including market presence, capabilities, and cultural fit, ensures that the right partners are brought on board. Through comprehensive onboarding and training programmes, coupled with ongoing support and communication, companies can empower their channel partners to drive sales, deliver value to customers, and contribute to the overall success of the channel strategy.

CHAPTER 5

PARTNER RELATIONSHIP MANAGEMENT

In the dynamic landscape of channel management, building and maintaining strong relationships with channel partners is indeed paramount to driving success and achieving long-term growth. As you mentioned, partner relationship management (PRM) encompasses the strategies, processes, and tools that companies employ to foster collaboration, align goals, and optimise the performance of their channel partners. This chapter's exploration of the key elements of effective PRM, including building strong partnerships, facilitating communication and collaboration, managing channel conflicts, and implementing rewarding and incentivising programmes, is crucial for understanding how to navigate the complexities of channel partnerships.

Building strong relationships with channel partners is the foundation of successful PRM. Palmatier et al. (2006)

emphasise that the quality of the relationship between a company and its channel partners is a critical driver of channel performance and long-term success. Strong partner relationships are characterised by trust, commitment, and mutual value creation (Morgan & Hunt, 1994). To build these strong relationships, companies must establish clear expectations and goals for the partnership, define roles and responsibilities, set performance metrics and targets, and establish clear lines of communication and feedback (Geyskens et al., 1999). By creating a shared understanding of the partnership's objectives and expectations, companies can lay the groundwork for a collaborative and productive relationship.

Demonstrating a commitment to the partner's success is another key aspect of building strong relationships. Moorman et al. (1992) suggest that companies that show a genuine interest in their partners' goals, challenges, and opportunities are more likely to foster trust and loyalty. This can involve providing training and support, sharing market insights and best practices, and investing in joint marketing and sales efforts to help partners grow their businesses. For example, a software company looking to strengthen its relationships with resellers may offer extensive product training, co-branded marketing materials, and lead generation support to help partners effectively sell and promote its solutions. By demonstrating a commitment to the partners' success, the company can build trust and encourage partners to invest more time and resources into the partnership.

Effective communication and collaboration are also essential for maintaining strong and productive partner relationships. Anderson and Narus (1990) point out that open and frequent communication helps build trust, resolve conflicts, and facilitate joint problem-solving and decision-making. Companies should establish regular communication channels and processes to keep partners informed, engaged, and aligned with their goals and strategies. Partner portals or extranets can be effective tools for facilitating communication and collaboration, providing a centralised hub for partners to access product information, marketing resources, training materials, and support services (Mirani et al., 2001). Regular performance reviews and feedback sessions are also important for providing partners with constructive feedback, recognising their achievements, and setting goals for the future (Jap, 1999).

Managing channel conflicts is another critical component of PRM. Channel conflicts can arise from various sources, such as price discrepancies, territory encroachment, or resource allocation, and can erode trust, damage relationships, and undermine the overall performance of the channel network if left unmanaged (Coughlan et al., 2006). To effectively manage channel conflicts, companies must establish clear policies and guidelines for partner conduct and collaboration, provide partners with clear communication and escalation processes to report and resolve conflicts and foster a culture of collaboration and shared goals among partners (Gilliland, 2004; Siguaw et al., 1998).

Finally, rewarding, and incentivising channel partners is a powerful tool for driving partner engagement, performance, and loyalty. Gilliland (2003) points out that effective incentive programmes can motivate partners to invest time and resources into promoting and selling the company's products or services. Tiered programmes that offer increasing levels of benefits and support based on the partner's performance and commitment to the relationship, performance-based rewards tied to specific goals or milestones, and non-monetary rewards such as public recognition or exclusive training opportunities can all be effective strategies for incentivising partners (Kalyanam & Brar, 2009; Viio & Grönroos, 2016).

In conclusion, partner relationship management is a critical component of channel management that requires a strategic and proactive approach. By building strong relationships, facilitating communication and collaboration, managing conflicts, and implementing effective reward and incentive programmes, companies can create a channel network that is more aligned, engaged, and motivated to drive results. As the business landscape continues to evolve and competition intensifies, prioritising PRM and continuously improving their approach will be essential for companies looking to succeed through indirect sales channels.

Understanding the Role of Channel Partners

The value channel partners contribute at every stage of the customer journey, regardless of whether they operate as distributors, resellers, retailers, or value-added service providers.

No matter what type of channel partner you may be, whether it is a distributor, reseller, retailer, or provider of value-added services, channel partners bring unique value at every stage of the customer journey.

At all stages of the customer journey, channel partners play an important role in delivering unique value to the company, whether they act as distributors, resellers, retailers, or value-added service providers.

There is no doubt that channel partners, whether they are distributors, resellers, retailers, or value-added service providers, contribute significantly to the success of the customer journey at every stage.

In every phase of the customer journey, whether they deal with distributors, resellers, retailers, or value-added service providers, channel partners contribute a unique level of value to the customer experience.

It does not matter whether or not channel partners operate as distributors, resellers, retailers, or value-added service providers; the fact is that channel partners contribute unique value to the customer journey at every stage.

Channel partners provide a unique value at each stage of the customer journey, whether they are acting as distributors, resellers, retailers, or value-added service providers of the products and services they provide.

Channel partners join the customer journey in a variety of ways, including as distributors, resellers, retailers, or value-added service providers. Each offers unique value for the customer at every stage of the journey.

In any situation, channel partners play a valuable role in helping customers at every stage of their customer journey, regardless of whether they operate as wholesalers, resellers, retailers, or value-added service providers.

Building Trust and Collaboration

In contrast, collaboration refers to engaging partners as strategic allies in pursuit of common goals and objectives through strategic alliances.

As a result of collaboration, partners are able to engage with each other as strategic allies to accomplish a common goal or objective.

When it comes to collaboration, on the other hand, allies are engaged as strategic allies in the pursuit of common goals and objectives.

The concept of collaboration refers to the process by which partners work together as strategic allies in order to attain common goals and objectives.

As for collaboration, it is an activity that involves engaging partners as strategic allies in pursuit of common goals and objectives.

As for collaboration, it is an activity that involves engaging partners as strategic allies in pursuit of common goals and objectives.

Collaboration refers to the process of bringing together partners as strategic allies so that they can contribute to the achievement of common goals and objectives.

The concept of collaboration, on the other hand, involves bringing partners together in a collaborative project to achieve common objectives and goals.

The term collaboration is also used to describe the process of engaging partners as strategic allies towards achieving common goals and achieving objectives together.

In contrast, collaboration refers to bringing together partners in a strategic alliance in order to follow common goals and objectives.

Collaboration, on the other hand, involves engaging partners as strategic allies in pursuit of common goals and objectives through mutually beneficial partnerships.

Building Strong Partner Relationships

Some key points about building strong partner relationships as the foundation of successful partner relationship management. Palmatier et al. (2006) indeed emphasise that the quality of the relationship between a company and its channel partners is a critical driver of channel performance and long-term success. Trust, commitment, and mutual value creation are essential characteristics of strong partner relationships, as noted by Morgan and Hunt (1994). Establishing clear expectations and goals for the partnership is crucial for laying the groundwork for a collaborative and productive relationship. Geyskens et al. (1999) suggest that defining roles and responsibilities, setting performance metrics and targets, and establishing clear lines of communication and feedback are important steps in this process. By creating a shared understanding of the partnership's objectives and expectations, companies can align their efforts and work towards common goals. Demonstrating a commitment to the partner's success is another important aspect of building strong relationships. Moorman et al. (1992) highlight that companies showing genuine interest in their partners' goals, challenges, and opportunities are more likely to foster trust and loyalty. Providing training and support, sharing market insights and best practices, and investing in joint marketing and sales efforts are practical ways to demonstrate this commitment and help partners grow their businesses.

For example, a software company strengthening its relationships with resellers by offering extensive product training, co-branded marketing materials, and lead generation support illustrates how companies can demonstrate their commitment to their partners' success. By providing these resources and support, the software company can help its partners effectively sell and promote its solutions, ultimately benefiting both parties. These actions build trust and encourage partners to reciprocate by investing more time and resources into the partnership.

Building strong partner relationships requires ongoing effort and investment from both the company and its channel partners. Regular communication, performance reviews, and opportunities for feedback and collaboration are essential for maintaining and growing these relationships over time. By prioritising partner relationship management and consistently demonstrating a commitment to mutual success, companies can create a strong foundation for long-term, profitable partnerships.

It's important to note that while the examples and strategies discussed here are based on research and best practices, the specific approaches to building strong partner relationships may vary depending on the industry, market, and individual partnerships. Companies should tailor their partner relationship management strategies to their unique context and continuously monitor and adapt their approach based on feedback and results.

In addition to the points, there are a few other factors that can contribute to building strong partner relationships:

1. **Mutual trust and respect:** Fostering a culture of mutual trust and respect is essential for building strong partnerships. This involves being transparent, following through on commitments,

and treating partners as valuable contributors to the business.

2. **Flexibility and adaptability:** Market conditions, customer needs, and partner circumstances can change over time. Being flexible and adaptable in the face of these changes can help maintain strong relationships and ensure that the partnership remains mutually beneficial.

3. **Conflict resolution:** Despite best efforts, conflicts can arise in any partnership. Having clear processes and protocols for addressing and resolving conflicts in a fair and timely manner can help maintain trust and prevent minor issues from escalating into major problems.

4. **Continuous improvement:** Regularly assessing the partnership's performance, seeking feedback, and identifying areas for improvement can help strengthen the relationship over time. This may involve updating goals, adjusting strategies, or providing additional resources and support as needed.

By incorporating these factors alongside the strategies you've highlighted, companies can create a strong foundation for successful, long-lasting partnerships that drive growth and success for all parties involved.

Communication and Collaboration

The importance of effective communication and collaboration in maintaining strong and productive partner relationships is paramount... As Anderson and Narus (1990) point out, open and frequent communication is crucial for building trust, resolving conflicts, and facilitating joint problem-solving and decision-making. Establishing regular communication channels and processes is essential for keeping partners informed, engaged, and aligned with the company's goals and strategies.

Partner portals or extranets are indeed effective tools for facilitating communication and collaboration, as mentioned by Mirani et al. (2001). These online platforms serve as a centralised hub for partners to access important information, such as product details, marketing resources, training materials, and support services. By providing a single point of access for these resources, partner portals can help streamline communication and ensure that all partners have the information they need to effectively sell and support the company's products or services.

Moreover, partner portals can enable collaboration through features such as discussion forums, project management tools, and document sharing. These features allow partners to share ideas, best practices, and success stories, fostering a sense of community and collaboration within the channel network. For example, a customer goods company using a partner portal to share sales data, market research, and promotional plans with its distributors and retailers can also encourage partners to share their feedback and insights, leading to more informed decision-making and better alignment of marketing efforts.

Regular performance reviews and feedback sessions are another critical aspect of communication and collaboration in partner relationship management.

As Jap (1999) suggests, providing partners with constructive feedback and recognising their achievements can help build trust, motivation, and continuous improvement. Scheduling regular review meetings with partners to discuss performance metrics, identify areas for improvement, and set goals for the future is an effective way to ensure that the partnership remains on track and that both parties are working towards common objectives.

During these performance reviews, it's important to focus on both quantitative and qualitative metrics. Quantitative metrics, such as sales targets, market share, and customer satisfaction scores, provide a clear picture of the partnership's performance and help identify areas for improvement. Qualitative metrics, such as partner feedback, collaboration quality, and alignment with company values, can provide valuable insights into the health of the relationship and highlight opportunities for strengthening the partnership. In addition to regular performance reviews, ongoing communication and collaboration can be facilitated through various channels, such as:

1. **Regular newsletters or email updates:** Keeping partners informed about new products, promotions, industry trends, and company news can help maintain engagement and alignment.

2. **Training and development programmes:** Offering ongoing training and development opportunities can help partners stay up-to-date with product knowledge, sales techniques, and market trends while also fostering a sense of investment in the partnership.

3. **Partner events and conferences:** Hosting events or conferences specifically for channel partners can provide opportunities for networking, sharing best practices, and strengthening relationships between the company and its partners, as well as among partners themselves.

4. **Joint planning and goal-setting:** Collaborating with partners to develop joint business plans, set shared goals, and align strategies can help ensure that both parties are working towards the same objectives and can lead to more effective allocation of resources and efforts.

By leveraging these various communication and collaboration channels, companies can create a strong, supportive ecosystem that empowers partners to succeed and drives long-term, mutually beneficial relationships. It's important to remember that effective communication and collaboration require ongoing effort and investment from both the company and its partners and that the specific strategies and channels used may need to be adapted over time based on the evolving needs and preferences of the partnership.

Providing Training and Support

In addition to initial training, ongoing support and resources are essential for partners to be able to deal with challenges, overcome obstacles, and take advantage of opportunities as they arise.

It is crucial for partners to receive ongoing support and resources as well as initial training in order to address challenges, overcome obstacles, and take advantage of opportunities.

In addition to the initial training, partners should have access to ongoing support and resources to help them overcome challenges, overcome obstacles, and capitalise on opportunities as they arise.

As well as initial training, ongoing support and resources are essential for assisting partners in addressing challenges, overcoming obstacles, and taking advantage of opportunities as they present themselves.

Additionally, to enhance the performance of the partners in their roles, ongoing support and resources are critical components that help them address challenges, overcome obstacles, and take advantage of opportunities as they arise.

It's imperative for the partner community to have both initial training with the ability to offer support and resources to assist them in overcoming challenges, overcoming obstacles, and leveraging opportunities when they arise in order to succeed.

Along with initial training, ongoing support and resources are essential to assisting partners in overcoming challenges, succeeding over obstacles, and taking advantage of opportunities when they arise by joining in the efforts and leveraging assets available to them.

It is very important to maintain regular communication with employees, with topics ranging from product updates, market trends, sales initiatives, and feedback regarding performance being covered.

Resolving Conflicts and Addressing Challenges

In order to effectively resolve conflicts, it is important to understand the root causes of the conflict, acknowledge their divergent perspectives, and find a common ground for resolution.

A successful conflict resolution process involves understanding the underlying causes of conflict, recognising the differing perspectives of the two sides, and identifying a common ground for resolving the conflict.

In order to resolve conflicts effectively, one must understand the underlying causes, acknowledge different perspectives, and seek to find some common ground where both parties can agree.

In order to resolve conflict effectively, it is important to understand that there are many root causes behind conflicts, acknowledge the differing perspectives, and work together to find a solution.

As part of effective conflict resolution, it is essential to understand the root causes of conflicts, recognise diverse perspectives, and work towards finding a common ground for resolution.

As part of resolving conflicts effectively, one has to be able to understand their underlying causes, acknowledge their different perspectives, and find a middle ground.

A successful conflict resolution strategy emphasises understanding the root causes of conflict, acknowledging the difference in perspectives, and looking for a common ground for resolving conflict.

The resolution of conflicts requires an understanding of the conflict's root causes as well as an acknowledgement of the perspectives of those involved and the objective of reaching common ground in order to do so.

There are many elements that contribute to successful conflict resolution, including understanding the root causes of conflict, accepting diverse perspectives, and finding common ground with which to settle a conflict.

Managing Channel Conflicts

Managing channel conflicts, are a common challenge in partner relationship management. As Coughlan et al. (2006) note, channel conflicts can arise from various sources, such as price discrepancies, territory encroachment, or resource allocation. These conflicts can indeed erode trust, damage relationships, and undermine the overall performance of the channel network if left unmanaged.

Establishing clear policies and guidelines for partner conduct and collaboration is a crucial step in effectively managing channel conflicts. As Gilliland (2004) suggests, setting rules for pricing, territory management, and customer engagement can help minimise the potential for conflicts. By providing partners with a clear framework for how to operate within the channel network, companies can reduce ambiguity and ensure that all partners are playing by the same rules.

In addition to setting clear policies, providing partners with clear communication and escalation processes to report and resolve conflicts in a timely and fair manner is essential. When conflicts do arise, having a well-defined process for addressing them can help prevent minor issues from escalating into major problems that can damage the partnership. This process should involve open communication, active listening, and a focus on finding mutually beneficial solutions that maintain the integrity of the partnership.

Fostering a culture of collaboration and shared goals among partners is another effective strategy for managing channel conflicts, as Siguaw et al. (1998) suggest. By encouraging partners to work together towards common objectives, such as increasing market share or improving customer satisfaction, companies can create a more cooperative and supportive environment that reduces the likelihood of conflicts.

Aligning partners' incentives and rewards with the overall performance of the channel network is a powerful way to promote collaboration and shared goals. For example, a technology company implementing a joint marketing campaign that rewards partners for generating leads and sales across the entire product portfolio rather than just their own offerings can encourage partners to collaborate and support each other's efforts. By creating a shared goal and incentive structure, the company can foster a sense of teamwork and mutual benefit that helps reduce conflicts and drive overall channel performance.

Other strategies for managing channel conflicts and fostering collaboration include:

1. **Regular communication and feedback:** Encouraging open and honest communication among partners and providing regular opportunities for feedback can help identify potential conflicts early and facilitate collaborative problem-solving.

2. **Partner segmentation:** Segmenting partners based on their capabilities, market focus, or other relevant criteria can help reduce conflicts

by ensuring that partners are not directly competing for the same customers or resources.

3. **Conflict resolution training:** Providing partners with training on effective conflict resolution techniques, such as active listening, empathy, and problem-solving, can help them better navigate and resolve conflicts when they arise.

4. **Neutral third-party mediation:** In cases where conflicts cannot be resolved through direct communication and collaboration, engaging a neutral third-party mediator can help facilitate a fair and mutually beneficial resolution.

Ultimately, managing channel conflicts requires a proactive and strategic approach that prioritises clear communication, collaboration, and alignment of goals and incentives. By establishing a strong foundation of trust and mutual benefit and by providing partners with the tools and support they need to navigate conflicts effectively, companies can create a more harmonious and productive channel network that drives long-term success for all parties involved.

Rewarding and Incentivising Channel Partners

Rewarding and incentivising channel partners is indeed a critical component of partner relationship management, as it helps motivate partners to invest time and resources into promoting and selling the company's products or services. As Gilliland (2003) points out, effective incentive programmes can drive partner loyalty, performance, and alignment with the company's goals and strategies.

A tiered programme that offers increasing levels of benefits and support based on the partner's performance and commitment to the relationship is a common approach to rewarding and incentivising partners. As you mentioned, a software company may offer bronze, silver, and gold tiers to its resellers based on their sales volume, customer satisfaction ratings, and technical certifications. By providing more generous discounts, marketing support, and access to exclusive resources and events to higher-tier partners, the company can encourage partners to strive for better performance and deeper engagement with the brand.

Tiered programmes can also help create a sense of exclusivity and aspiration among partners as they work to achieve higher levels of recognition and rewards. This can foster healthy competition and motivation within the channel network, driving partners to continuously improve their performance and commitment to the partnership.

Performance-based rewards, such as bonuses, rebates, or marketing development funds (MDF), are another effective incentive strategy, as highlighted by Kalyanam and Brar (2009). By tying rewards directly to specific goals or milestones, such as sales growth, new customer acquisition, or product certification, companies can encourage partners to focus on the activities that drive the most value for the business.

For example, a telecommunications company offering a quarterly bonus to partners who exceed their sales targets or generate a certain number of new customer contracts can create a clear link between partner performance and rewards. This direct connection can be a powerful motivator for partners to go above and beyond in promoting and selling the company's services.

It's important to note that performance-based rewards should be designed with fairness and transparency in mind. The goals and milestones should be achievable, relevant to the partner's role and capabilities, and clearly communicated in advance. The rewards themselves should be meaningful and commensurate with the level of effort and achievement required to earn them.

In addition to financial incentives, non-monetary rewards such as public recognition, exclusive training and development opportunities, or invitations to special events and conferences can be highly effective in building emotional connections and a sense of partnership between the company and its channel partners, as suggested by Viio and Grönroos (2016).

Public recognition, such as featuring high-performing partners in company newsletters, social media posts, or industry publications, can provide a powerful boost to a partner's reputation and credibility in the market. This recognition can also help attract new customers and partnership opportunities for the recognised partners.

Exclusive training and development opportunities, such as access to advanced product training, leadership workshops, or mentorship programmes, can help partners build their skills, knowledge, and capabilities, ultimately enabling them to better serve customers and drive sales. These opportunities can also demonstrate the company's commitment to the partner's long-term success and growth.

Invitations to special events and conferences, such as annual partner summits, industry tradeshows, or VIP customer events, can provide partners with valuable networking opportunities, exposure to new ideas and best practices, and a sense of belonging to a larger community of successful professionals. These experiences can help strengthen the emotional bond between the company and its partners, fostering greater loyalty and engagement over time.

Ultimately, the most effective incentive programmes are those that align with the company's goals and partners' motivations, creating a win-win situation that benefits both parties and drives long-term success. By combining financial and non-monetary rewards, and by designing programmes that are fair, transparent, and meaningful to partners, companies can create a powerful ecosystem of motivated, loyal, and high-performing channel partners.

It's worth noting that incentive programmes should be regularly reviewed and adapted based on feedback from partners, changes in market conditions, and evolving company priorities. By maintaining open lines of communication and being receptive to partner input, companies can ensure that their incentive programmes remain relevant, effective, and mutually beneficial over time.

Moreover, while rewards and incentives are important, they should be part of a larger partner relationship management strategy that also includes elements such as clear communication, joint planning and goal-setting, and continuous support and collaboration. By taking a holistic approach to partner engagement and success, companies can build strong, lasting relationships that drive growth and value creation for all parties involved.

Conclusion

In conclusion, partner relationship management is a critical component of channel management that requires a strategic and proactive approach. Building strong relationships with channel partners, facilitating communication and collaboration, managing channel conflicts, and implementing effective reward and incentive programmes are all essential elements of successful PRM.

By investing in these areas and adopting a partner-centric mindset, companies can create a channel network that is more aligned, engaged, and motivated to drive results. Strong partner relationships based on trust, commitment, and shared goals can help companies navigate the challenges of the market, adapt to changing customer needs, and achieve long-term growth and profitability.

As the business landscape continues to evolve and competition intensifies, partner relationship management will only become more important for companies looking to succeed through indirect sales channels. By prioritising PRM and continuously improving their approach, companies can build a competitive advantage and create value for all stakeholders in the channel ecosystem.

CHAPTER 6

CHANNEL STRATEGY DEVELOPMENT

Introduction to Channel Strategy Development

A channel strategy, at its core, consists of crafting a roadmap that lays out how a company will reach its target markets, allocate resources, and collaborate with its channel partners in order to reach its business goals.

In the simplest of terms, channel strategy development is the process of developing a roadmap to outline how a company will reach the target markets it has identified, allocate resources, and collaborate with channel partners to achieve its objectives.

To develop a channel strategy, it is essential for an organisation to create a roadmap that outlines how it plans to reach its target markets, allocate resources to reach them, and collaborate with the channel partners to do so.

At its core, the development of a channel strategy involves creating a framework that outlines how a business will reach its target markets, allocate its resources, and collaborate with channel partners to achieve its goals.

A company's channel strategy entails the creation of a roadmap that outlines the steps it will take in order to reach its target markets, allocate resources, and collaborate with channel partners in order to implement a plan.

It is essential to understand that the development of a channel strategy is about defining how a company will reach its target markets, allocate resources, and collaborate with a wide range of channel partners.

To develop a channel strategy, a company must develop a roadmap that outlines how it intends to reach its target markets, communicate with its partners, and allocate resources to accomplish the objectives of the strategy.

In order to develop effective channel strategies, a business must create a roadmap that specifies how it will reach its target markets, allocate resources, and work in partnership with the company's channel partners.

An effective channel strategy is essentially the creation of a roadmap that clearly outlines how a company will reach its target markets, allocate resources, and collaborate with channel partners as part of an overall plan to reach those markets.

The concept of channel strategy development can be divided into three distinct components. The first of which involves developing a roadmap outlining how a company will reach its target markets, allocate resources, and collaborate with channel partners.

Aligning Channel Strategy with Business Objectives

As a result of this alignment, every decision made in the development of the company's channel strategy, from choosing the distribution channels to partnering with intermediaries, is driven by a clear understanding of how the decision will contribute to the company's overarching goals.

This alignment ensures that every decision made during the development of the company's channel strategy-from selecting distribution channels to reach out to intermediaries-will be driven by a clear understanding of how it will contribute to the company's overarching objectives.

It is essential that the company's channel strategy development is aligned with its overarching objectives in order to ensure that every decision made in this respect-from deciding on distribution channels to partnering with intermediaries contributes to the achievement of the company's goals.

Through this alignment, every decision made in the development of the channel strategy- from choosing distribution channels to partnering with intermediaries-is driven by a clear understanding of how it will assist the company in achieving its overarching objectives.

Throughout all stages of the development of a channel strategy, all decisions are driven by a clear understanding of how those decisions will help the company attain its overarching objectives, which ensures that every decision made in the development of a channel strategy will contribute to the achievement of those objectives.

By aligning the channel strategy development process with the overarching objectives of the company, every decision made in terms of distribution channels, partnership with intermediaries and development of distribution channels is driven by a clear understanding of how it contributes to the company's ultimate goal.

The alignment of these objectives ensures that whenever a decision regarding a channel strategy is being made, from choosing distribution channels to partnering with intermediaries, it is done with a clear understanding of how it will contribute to the company's overarching objectives.

In this way, every decision made within the channel strategy development - such as choosing distribution channels or partnering with intermediaries - is driven by a clear appreciation of how it will contribute to the company's overarching objectives, ensuring a consistent approach to channel strategy development.

Every decision made in the development of a channel strategy -- from selecting distribution channels to entering into partnerships with intermediaries -- is driven by a clear understanding of how it will contribute to the company's overarching objectives, and every decision is based on that understanding.

This alignment ensures that every decision made in the development of the channel strategy—from selecting distribution channels to partnering with intermediaries—is driven by a clear understanding of how it can contribute to the company's overarching objectives in order to successfully execute the strategy.

Segmenting Target Markets

An effective segmentation strategy involves the analysis of demographic, psychographic, geographic, and behavioural data to identify groups of customers with similar characteristics and purchasing behaviours, resulting in a better understanding of the customer.

Identifying groups of customers based on similar characteristics and behaviours is one of the most effective ways to segment customers by using demographic, psychographic, geographic, and behavioural data.

The ability to segment effectively involves the analysis of demographic, psychographic, geographical, and behavioural data in order to identify groups of customers who share the same characteristics and have similar purchasing behaviours.

The purpose of effective segmentation is to identify groups of customers that have similar characteristics and purchasing patterns, determined by analysing demographic, psychographic, geographical, and behavioural data.

The process of segmentation involves analysing demographic information, psychographic data, geographic data, and behavioural data that are related to customers in order to identify groups of customers with similar characteristics and buying behaviours. There are several factors that go into effective segmentation, such as demographic, psychographic, geographic, and behavioural data, that help in identifying groups of customers who offer similar characteristics and purchasing behaviours.

Segmentation requires analysing demographic, psychographic, geographic, and behavioural data to identify groups of customers with similar characteristics and purchasing behaviours to determine which groups they belong to.

To segment your customers effectively, it is necessary to analyse demographic, psychographic, geographic, and behavioural information. This will allow us to identify groups of customers who have similar purchasing characteristics as well as similar behaviour patterns. To accomplish effective segmentation, demographic, psychographic, geographic, and behavioural data should be analysed to identify groups of customers with similar characteristics and purchasing behaviours that can be compared.

An effective segmentation programme involves the analysis of demographics, psychographics, demographic data, geographic data, and behavioural data to identify groups of customers with similar characteristics and purchasing behaviours in order to build effective marketing campaigns.

Evaluating Channel Options

While direct channels offer a greater level of control over the customer experience and brand messaging, they may also require significant investments in infrastructure and resources on the part of the brand.

There is no doubt that direct channels offer greater control over the customer experience and brand messaging, but they may also require substantial investments in infrastructure and resource allocation.

The direct channel offers greater control over the brand messaging and customer experience; however, it may require a considerable investment in infrastructure and resources to achieve significant results.

There can be a great deal of control over the customer experience and brand messaging when using direct channels. However, significant investments may be required in infrastructure and resources to effectively use direct channels.

It is likely that direct channels will provide greater control over the customer experience and brand messaging for your brand, however, they may also require a significant investment in infrastructure and resources.

Unlike direct marketing channels, direct marketing can offer greater control over the customer experience and brand messaging for a company, but it may also require a large investment of infrastructure and resources.

Although direct channels offer greater control over the customer experience and brand message, they may also require significant resources and infrastructure investments in order to succeed.

A direct channel provides greater control over the customer experience and the brand messaging of the brand than one that uses indirect channels, but it may require a significant investment in infrastructure and resources.

Although direct marketing channels can be advantageous in terms of their ability to deliver a memorable brand experience for customers and control over brand messaging, large investments in infrastructure and resources may be necessary.

Compared with direct channels, direct channels can provide greater control over the customer experience and brand messaging but may require significant investments in the infrastructure and other resources to succeed.

Selecting Channel Partners

If you want to select the right partners, you have to take into account their ability to align with the company's brand values, customer service standards, and long-term strategic objectives.

It is important to carefully consider the partner's ability to align with the company's brand values, customer service standards, and long-term strategic objectives when selecting a new partner.

The process of selecting the right partner requires careful consideration of how well the company's brand values, customer service standards, and long-term strategic objectives can be aligned with the partner's organisation.

In selecting the right partners for your business, you must carefully consider their ability to align with the brand values of your business, customer service standards, and long-term strategic objectives of the organisation.

The selection of the right business partners requires a lot of careful consideration, including the ability to align with the company's brand values, standards of customer service, and long-term strategic goals.

If the company is looking for the right partners, it will need to carefully consider its ability to align its brand values, service standards, and long-term strategic objectives with the company's brand values and customer service standards.

There is a lot to consider when choosing the right partners for your organisation. You should carefully evaluate whether or not the company's brand values, customer service standards, and long-term strategic objectives are aligned with theirs.

It is important to carefully evaluate potential partners in terms of their alignment with the company's brand values, customer service standards, and long-term strategic objectives as part of the selection process.

The selection of the right partner is a big decision that requires a great deal of thought and care, as they must align with the brand values as well as the standards of customer service as well as the company's long-term strategic objectives.

Developing Channel Policies and Agreements

In channel agreements, the rights, responsibilities, and obligations of each party are formalised, outlining the terms and conditions of the engagement, as well as mechanisms for resolving disputes between the parties.

The channel agreement establishes the rights, responsibilities, and obligations of each party, as well as the terms of the engagement and the mechanisms for resolving any disputes between them.

As part of the channels agreements, the parties are formally defined as to their rights, responsibilities, and obligations, as well as the terms of engagement and mechanisms for resolving disputes.

A channel agreement specifies the rights, responsibilities, and obligations of both parties, as well as the terms of engagement and any dispute resolution mechanisms that will be applied.

As part of channel agreements, each party has the right to set its own rights, responsibilities, and obligations, outlining the terms of engagement and providing mechanisms for dispute resolution.

It is important to note that channel agreements lay out the rights, responsibilities, and obligations of each party, as well as the terms of engagement and other methods for resolving disputes.

Channel agreements are formal agreements that define the rights, responsibilities, and obligations of each party involved, as well as the terms of engagement and mechanisms for resolving any disputes.

This agreement formalises the rights, responsibilities, and obligations of each party, illustrating the terms of engagement and providing mechanisms for resolving disputes between the parties.

Essentially, channel agreements provide an outline of the rights, responsibilities, and obligations of each party and spell out the terms and conditions of their engagement, as well as the mechanisms through which disputes might be resolved.

Implementing Channel Training and Support Programmes

It is not uncommon for training programmes to cover a wide range of topics, such as product features and benefits, sales techniques, market trends, and customer service protocols.

The topics that may be covered in a training programme may include a variety of topics, including product features and benefits, sales techniques, market trends, and customer service protocols.

Various topics may be covered during training programmes, including the features and benefits of a product, sales techniques, market trends, and protocols for customer service.

A range of topics may be discussed during a training programme, including features and benefits of the product, sales techniques, market trends, and customer service protocols, among others.

A training programme may cover a variety of topics, such as the features and benefits of the product, sales techniques, market trends, and customer service protocols, to name just a few.

The training programmes that are offered by companies and organisations can cover a wide range of topics, such as product features and benefits, sales techniques, market trends, and customer service protocols.

The training programmes that are offered by companies and organisations can cover a wide range of topics, such as product features and benefits, sales techniques, market trends, and customer service protocols.

It is common for training programmes to cover an assortment of topics, including product features and benefits, sales techniques, market trends, and customer service protocols.

Programmes of training may cover a range of topics, including product features and benefits, sales techniques, market trends, and customer service protocols, in addition to a variety of topics covered in training courses.

An organisation's training programmes may cover a wide range of topics, including product features, benefits, sales techniques, market trends, and customer service protocols, as well as evaluating customer feedback.

Monitoring and Evaluating Channel Performance

It is imperative that companies establish clear metrics and benchmarks for evaluating channel performance and monitor their progress against these goals on a regular basis.

It is imperative that companies establish clear benchmarks and metrics that can be used to evaluate channel performance and track progress against these goals on a regular basis.

In order to evaluate the performance of marketing channels, companies need to establish clearly defined metrics and benchmarks and monitor progress on achieving these goals on a regular basis.

A company should establish clear metrics and benchmarks for measuring channel performance and track the progress that is being made against these goals on a regular basis.

Defining clear metrics and benchmarks for evaluating channel performance is imperative, and companies should constantly monitor progress towards their goals against these metrics and benchmarks.

Companies need to establish clear metrics and benchmarks for evaluating channel performance and track their progress toward these goals on a regular basis.

In order to evaluate channel performance, companies must establish clear metrics and benchmarks for measuring it and regularly track their progress against these goals in order to ensure consistency.

In order to evaluate channel performance, companies need to establish clear metrics that allow them to track their progress against these goals on a regular basis.

The company must determine clear metrics and benchmarks for evaluating the channel performance as well as monitor progress towards these goals regularly during the evaluation process.

Adapting Channel Strategies to Market Dynamics

A company that stays ahead of the curve can position itself for success and capitalise on evolving market trends by positioning itself for success.

It is essential for companies to stay ahead of the curve in order to position themselves for success and to take advantage of evolving market trends.

A business can position itself for success and capitalise on evolving market trends by staying ahead of the curve and positioning itself for success.

Keeping up with the latest market trends is one of the best ways for companies to stay ahead of the curve and leverage evolving market trends to their advantage.

Staying ahead of the curve is a good way for companies to position themselves for success in the future and capitalise on emerging market trends.

Staying ahead of the curve is a good way for companies to position themselves for success in the future and capitalise on emerging market trends.

Being able to stay ahead of the curve will enable companies to position themselves for success and capture market trends as they evolve.

It is crucial for companies to stay ahead of the curve in order to position themselves for future success and capitalise on the market trends that are evolving.

As long as companies stay ahead of the curve and capitalise on evolving market trends, they can be sure to position themselves for success and to be successful in the future.

Businesses that are able to position themselves for success and capitalise on changing market trends can position themselves for success by staying ahead of the curve.

It is essential that companies stay ahead of the curve in order to gain a competitive advantage and capitalise on the changing trends in the market.

Conclusion

The purpose of this chapter is to provide a foundation for subsequent discussion of the strategies and tactics of channel management, so that companies will be able to navigate the complexities of channel management, and maximise their distribution channels' opportunities.

In the following chapters, we will explore channel management strategies and tactics to help companies navigate the complexities of channel management and strategically capitalise on opportunities within their distribution channels by providing a foundation for future discussions.

A foundation is laid by this chapter for subsequent discussions on channel management strategies and tactics in order to provide companies with the knowledge and tools to navigate the complexities of channel management as well as capitalise on the opportunities within it.

Chapter one of this book provides the reader with a solid foundation for discussing strategy and tactics for channel management, which give companies a better understanding of how to navigate the complexity of channel management, and make the most of opportunities within their distribution channels.

Throughout the rest of the chapter, we provide a framework for additional discussions on channel management strategies and tactics, equipping companies with the necessary skills to navigate the complexities of channel management and capitalise on opportunities within their distribution channels.

This chapter serves as a foundation for the discussion that follows on channel management strategies and tactics, enabling companies to gain a more comprehensive understanding of their channel management capabilities while maximising the opportunities available within their distribution channels.

Throughout the chapter, there is a foundation for a discussion focusing on channel management strategies and tactics that will be used to empower companies to navigate the complexities of channel management and capitalise on opportunities within their distribution channels.

There is much to be discussed in subsequent chapters, but this chapter provides a solid foundation for further discussion of company and channel management strategies and tactics, enabling businesses to navigate the complexities of managing channels and to take advantage of opportunities within them.

We will use Chapter 1 to lay the foundation for discussions that follow channel management strategies and tactics, providing companies with the tools needed to successfully navigate the complexities of channel management and maximise their distribution channels' potential.

CHAPTER 7

PERFORMANCE MEASUREMENT AND EVALUATION

Key Metrics for Channel Performance Evaluation

Effective channel performance evaluation relies on the measurement of key metrics and indicators that provide insights into various aspects of channel effectiveness and efficiency.

This section explores the key metrics commonly used for channel performance evaluation, categorising them into different dimensions such as sales performance, partner performance, and customer satisfaction.

Sales performance metrics are fundamental for assessing the revenue generation capabilities of distribution channels. Key metrics in this category include total sales revenue, sales growth rate, sales conversion rate, and average order value.

By tracking these metrics over time, companies can evaluate the effectiveness of their sales efforts and identify opportunities for revenue optimisation.

Partner performance metrics focus on assessing the contribution of channel partners to overall channel performance. Metrics in this category may include partner revenue contribution, partner profitability, partner satisfaction scores, and partner engagement levels.

By evaluating partner performance, companies can identify top-performing partners, nurture strategic alliances, and address any performance issues or gaps.

Customer satisfaction metrics are critical for gauging the effectiveness of distribution channels in meeting customer needs and expectations. Metrics such as Net Promoter Score (NPS), customer retention rate, and customer lifetime value provide insights into customer loyalty, satisfaction, and advocacy.

By monitoring these metrics, companies can identify areas for improvement, prioritise customer-centric initiatives, and enhance overall customer experience.

Key Performance Indicators (KPIs)

A. Defining Relevant KPIs.

1. **Financial metrics** (revenue, profit margin, cost per acquisition, etc.)

2. **Operational metrics** (service level agreements, lead times, defect rates, etc.)

3. **Customer experience metrics** (satisfaction scores, net promoter score, churn rate, etc.)

B. Setting KPI Targets

1. Benchmarking against industry standards

2. Aligning with overall business objectives

3. Ensuring targets are achievable but drive improvement

C. Communicating And Cascading KPIs.

1. Gaining alignment and buy-in from stakeholders

2. Translating high-level KPIs to partner/channel-specific metrics

3. Providing tools and dashboards for tracking performance

Monitoring Channel Performance

A. Establishing data collection and reporting processes

1. Determining data sources and integration requirements

   2. Defining reporting frequency and format

   3. Assigning roles and responsibilities for data management

B. Analysing Performance Trends And Variances.

   1. Comparing actual results to targets

   2. Identifying root causes of underperformance

   3. Recognising and replicating best practices

C. Conducting Regular Business Reviews

   1. Preparing comprehensive performance reports

   2. Facilitating constructive dialogue with partners/ channel members

   3. Making data-driven decisions and action plans

Assessing Partner Effectiveness

A. Segmenting Partners Based On Value And Strategic Fit

   1. Considering financial contribution and growth potential

   2. Evaluating alignment with target markets and offerings

   3. Assessing capabilities and level of engagement

B. Developing Partner Scorecards And Dashboards.

   1. Incorporating KPIs and other strategic criteria

   2. Assigning weights based on relative importance

   3. Enabling objective comparison and ranking of partners

C. Linking Performance To Rewards And Consequences.

1. Defining incentives, rebates, marketing funds, etc.

2. Establishing a formal joint business planning process

3. Pruning underperforming partners when necessary

Continuous Improvement and Optimisation

A. Soliciting Feedback From Partners And Customers.

1. Conducting partner satisfaction and engagement surveys

2. Monitoring customer sentiment and loyalty metrics

3. Proactively seeking input on improvement opportunities

B. Sharing Best Practices Across The Channel

1. Communicating success stories and case studies

2. Facilitating knowledge transfer and collaboration

3. Providing training and development resources

C. Piloting New Initiatives And Measuring Impact.

1. Developing business cases and ROI projections

2. Designing pilots with clear success criteria

3. Rapidly iterating and scaling based on results

The key themes are defining clear and relevant metrics, setting appropriate targets, monitoring and assessing performance in a structured way, using insights to drive decision-making and improvement initiatives, and continuously optimising the channel to adapt to changing market conditions and customer needs. By taking a comprehensive and proactive approach to performance measurement and evaluation, organisations can get the most value from their channel partnerships and investments.

Performance Evaluation Tools and Techniques

In addition to key metrics, companies leverage a variety of tools and techniques to conduct channel performance evaluations effectively. This section explores some of the commonly used tools and techniques for channel performance evaluation, ranging from basic spreadsheet analysis to sophisticated data analytics and business intelligence solutions.

Basic spreadsheet analysis involves the use of spreadsheet software such as Microsoft Excel to collect, organise, and analyse channel performance data.

While relatively simple, spreadsheet analysis can be effective for small to medium-sized businesses with limited resources and data complexity.

Companies can create custom reports, dashboards, and charts to visualise performance metrics and identify trends and patterns.

Advanced analytics tools and techniques, such as data mining, predictive modelling, and machine learning algorithms, offer more sophisticated capabilities for channel performance evaluation.

These tools enable companies to analyse large volumes of data, uncover hidden insights, and generate actionable recommendations for improving channel effectiveness and efficiency.

By leveraging advanced analytics, companies can gain a competitive edge by making data-driven decisions and optimising channel strategies in real-time.

Furthermore, benchmarking is a valuable technique for comparing channel performance against industry standards or competitors' performance. By benchmarking key performance metrics, companies can identify areas of strength and weakness relative to peers and industry benchmarks, enabling them to set realistic performance targets and identify opportunities for improvement.

Aligning Incentives and Objectives

By aligning incentives with business objectives, companies are able to create a win-win situation where both parties are able to benefit from their partnership in the long run.

A win-win scenario can be created by aligning incentives with business objectives in order to create a win-win situation where both parties stand to benefit from the partnership in the long run.

Creating a win-win scenario for both parties is possible by aligning incentives with business objectives, which can create a win-win situation for both parties and benefit both parties in the long run.

Companies can achieve a win-win scenario by aligning incentives with their business objectives and creating a situation where both parties will benefit from their partnership based on the alignment of incentives. Incorporating incentives into business objectives can help companies create a win-win scenario where both parties stand to profit from their partnership if the incentives are aligned with business objectives. By aligning incentives with the company's business objectives, companies can create a scenario where both parties stand to benefit from the partnership by creating a win-win scenario.

If companies align their incentives with their business objectives, then they can create a win-win scenario where both parties will rise to the occasion and benefit from their partnership as a whole.

In the event that incentive programmes are aligned with a company's long-term business objectives, companies can create a win-win situation where both parties will reap the benefits of their relationship.

By aligning incentives with the goals of a company, it can be created a win-win scenario in which both parties will benefit from the partnership and this will lead to a win-win outcome.

In order to ensure that business objectives are aligned with incentives, businesses can create a win-win scenario where both parties feel that their partnership will benefit both of them.

Strategies for Optimising Channel Performance

Optimising channel performance requires a strategic approach that encompasses a range of initiatives and strategies aimed at enhancing channel effectiveness and efficiency. This section explores some of the strategies commonly employed by companies to optimise channel performance, including channel segmentation, partner incentives, and process optimisation. Channel segmentation involves dividing the target market into distinct segments based on factors such as geographic location, demographic characteristics, or purchasing behaviour. By segmenting the market, companies can tailor their channel strategies and initiatives to meet the unique needs and preferences of different customer segments, thereby maximising channel effectiveness and ROI.

Partner incentives play a crucial role in motivating channel partners to achieve desired performance outcomes. Companies can design incentive programmes that reward partners for achieving sales targets, driving customer loyalty, or participating in training and development initiatives. By aligning incentives with business objectives, companies can incentivise desired behaviours and drive mutual success within the distribution channel.

Process optimisation focuses on streamlining channel management processes to improve efficiency and reduce costs. This may involve automating manual tasks, such as order processing or inventory management, to free up time and resources for more value-added activities. By optimising processes, companies can enhance channel performance, minimise errors, and improve overall operational efficiency.

Furthermore, continuous monitoring and performance feedback are essential for identifying performance gaps and opportunities for improvement. By regularly reviewing channel performance metrics and providing timely feedback to channel partners, companies can foster a culture of accountability, collaboration, and continuous improvement within the distribution channel. Optimising channel performance necessitates a multifaceted approach that encompasses various strategies tailored to the specific needs and dynamics of the distribution channels.

This section delves deeper into some of the strategies commonly employed by companies to enhance channel performance.

Channel Segmentation: Channel segmentation involves dividing the target market into distinct segments based on factors such as geographic location, demographic characteristics, or purchasing behaviour. By understanding the unique needs and preferences of different customer segments, companies can tailor their channel strategies to better serve each segment. For example, high-value customers may require personalised service through direct channels, while cost-conscious customers may prefer the convenience and affordability of indirect channels. By segmenting the market and aligning channel strategies accordingly, companies can optimise channel performance and maximise customer satisfaction.

Partner Incentives: Motivating channel partners to achieve desired performance outcomes is essential for driving channel effectiveness and success. Companies can design incentive programmes that reward partners for achieving sales targets, driving customer loyalty, or participating in training and development initiatives. These incentives can take various forms, such as monetary bonuses, rebates, discounts, or recognition programmes. By aligning incentives with business objectives and partner interests, companies can encourage desired behaviours, foster partner engagement, and drive mutual success within the distribution channel.

Process Optimisation: Streamlining channel management processes is crucial for improving efficiency, reducing costs, and enhancing overall channel performance. Companies can identify and eliminate bottlenecks, redundancies, and inefficiencies in key processes such as order management, inventory replenishment, and customer support. Automation technologies, such as enterprise resource planning (ERP) systems, customer relationship management (CRM) software, and supply chain management (SCM) solutions, can automate routine tasks, improve workflow efficiency, and enhance data accuracy. By optimising processes, companies can streamline operations, minimise errors, and improve the overall customer experience.

Best Practices for Channel Performance Evaluation

Effective channel performance evaluation relies on best practices that enable companies to maximise the value of performance data and drive actionable insights. This section explores some of the best practices for channel performance evaluation, including data quality assurance, stakeholder collaboration, and performance benchmarking. Data quality assurance is fundamental for ensuring the accuracy, reliability, and integrity of channel performance data. Companies should establish data governance processes and protocols to maintain data quality standards, including data validation, cleansing, and normalisation. By investing in data quality assurance, companies can minimise errors and biases in

Effective channel performance evaluation relies on best practices that enable companies to maximise the value of performance data and drive actionable insights. This section explores some of the best practices for channel performance evaluation, including data quality assurance, stakeholder collaboration, and performance benchmarking.

Data Quality Assurance: Ensuring the accuracy, reliability, and integrity of channel performance data is fundamental for meaningful performance evaluation. Companies should establish data governance processes and protocols to maintain data quality standards, including data validation, cleansing, and normalisation. By investing in data quality assurance, companies can minimise errors and biases in performance data, enabling more accurate analysis and decision-making.

Stakeholder Collaboration: Collaboration among stakeholders is essential for effective channel performance evaluation. Companies should involve key stakeholders, including channel partners, sales teams, marketing teams, and senior management, in the performance evaluation process. By fostering collaboration and communication, companies can gain diverse perspectives, identify blind spots, and ensure alignment with overall business objectives. Regular meetings, workshops, and cross-functional teams can facilitate collaboration and promote a shared understanding of channel performance goals and strategies.

Performance Benchmarking: Benchmarking channel performance against industry standards or competitors' performance is valuable for identifying areas of strength and weakness and setting realistic performance targets. Companies should regularly benchmark key performance metrics against industry benchmarks, peer benchmarks, or internal benchmarks. Benchmarking can provide valuable insights into market trends, best practices, and areas for improvement, enabling companies to continuously enhance channel performance and maintain a competitive edge.

Monitoring Partner Performance

In addition to quantitative metrics, companies should also consider qualitative factors such as partner engagement, collaboration, and satisfaction levels as well as quantitative metrics.

The company should not only focus on quantitative metrics but also take into consideration qualitative factors such as partner engagement, collaboration, and levels of satisfaction with the company.

Furthermore, companies should also take into account qualitative factors, such as the level of partner engagement, the degree of collaboration, and the degree of satisfaction with the partnership.

As part of determining how well their partners are engaged, their level of collaboration, and their level of satisfaction with the product or service, the company should also consider qualitative factors as well as quantitative metrics.

It is also necessary for the company to take into consideration both qualitative and quantitative factors when determining how well their partners are engaged, their level of collaboration, and their level of satisfaction when evaluating the quality of their services.

The company should not only pay attention to quantitative metrics, but also qualitative factors when determining how well their partners are engaged, how well they collaborate with them, and how much satisfaction they experience when dealing with them.

When evaluating the level of engagement, the level of collaboration, and the level of satisfaction for their partners, the company should also consider both qualitative factors as well as quantitative metrics in determining how well their partners are engaged.

Case Studies and Practical Insights

Real-world case studies and practical insights offer valuable lessons and inspiration for companies seeking to optimise channel performance. This section presents a selection of case studies and practical insights that illustrate successful strategies and best practices in channel performance evaluation and optimisation.

Case Study 1:

Company XYZ, a leading customer goods manufacturer, implemented a comprehensive channel performance evaluation framework to assess the effectiveness of its distribution channels and optimise its channel strategies. By leveraging data analytics tools and techniques, Company XYZ analysed sales performance, partner engagement, and customer satisfaction across its distribution channels. The company identified key performance metrics, such as sales conversion rates, customer retention rates, and partner profitability, and used them to measure and evaluate channel performance.

Through continuous monitoring and analysis, Company XYZ identified opportunities for improvement, such as optimising product assortment, enhancing partner training and support, and investing in digital marketing initiatives. By implementing these recommendations, Company XYZ was able to improve channel effectiveness, drive sales growth, and enhance customer satisfaction.

Practical Insight 1:

Regular performance reviews and feedback sessions are essential for maintaining accountability and driving continuous improvement within distribution channels. By establishing clear performance targets, providing timely feedback, and recognising top performers, companies can motivate channel partners to achieve desired outcomes and foster a culture of excellence and collaboration.

Case Study 2:

Company ABC, a global technology company, leveraged predictive analytics to forecast demand and optimise inventory levels across its distribution channels. By analysing historical sales data, market trends, and other relevant factors, Company ABC developed predictive models to anticipate changes in customer demand and adjust inventory levels accordingly. By optimising inventory levels, Company ABC was able to minimise stockouts, reduce excess inventory, and improve overall supply chain efficiency.

Practical Insight 2:

Predictive analytics can provide valuable insights into future channel performance and help companies anticipate changes in market dynamics, customer behaviour, and competitive landscape. By leveraging predictive analytics, companies can make proactive decisions, mitigate risks, and capitalise on emerging opportunities, thereby gaining a competitive edge in the marketplace.

Identify opportunities for improvement and implement strategies to enhance channel performance and drive sustainable growth and profitability.

Leveraging Data Analytics for Channel Performance Evaluation

Data analytics plays a crucial role in channel performance evaluation, enabling companies to derive actionable insights from large volumes of data and drive informed decision-making. This section explores the role of data analytics in channel performance evaluation and highlights some of the key techniques and tools used.

Descriptive Analytics: Descriptive analytics involves analysing historical data to understand past performance and identify trends and patterns. Companies can use descriptive analytics techniques, such as data visualisation, trend analysis, and cohort analysis, to gain insights into channel performance over time. By visualizing performance data in charts, graphs, and dashboards, companies can identify key trends, anomalies, and areas for further investigation.

Predictive Analytics: Predictive analytics involves using statistical algorithms and machine learning techniques to forecast future channel performance-based on historical data and other relevant factors. Companies can use predictive analytics models to identify emerging trends, anticipate changes in customer behaviour, and forecast sales performance. By leveraging predictive analytics, companies can anticipate market trends, identify opportunities, and make proactive decisions to optimise channel performance.

Prescriptive Analytics: Prescriptive analytics involves using advanced modelling techniques to recommend actions and strategies for improving channel performance. Companies can use prescriptive analytics models to identify the most effective channel strategies, optimise resource allocation, and address performance gaps. By generating actionable recommendations based on data analysis, prescriptive analytics empowers companies to make informed decisions and drive continuous improvement in channel performance.

Data Visualisation Tools: Data visualisation tools, such as Tableau, Power BI, and Google Data Studio, are essential for creating interactive dashboards and reports that visualise channel performance data. These tools allow companies to explore data visually, identify patterns, and communicate insights effectively. By creating interactive dashboards, companies can enable stakeholders to explore channel performance data dynamically and gain deeper insights into performance trends and patterns.

Advanced Analytics Platforms: Advanced analytics platforms, such as SAS, IBM Watson Analytics, and Microsoft Azure Machine Learning, provide advanced analytics capabilities, including predictive modelling, machine learning, and natural language processing. These platforms enable companies to build sophisticated analytics models, analyse complex data sets, and derive actionable insights. By leveraging advanced analytics platforms, companies can unlock the full potential of their data and drive innovation in channel performance evaluation.

Conclusion

In conclusion, performance measurement and evaluation play a critical role in ensuring the success and sustainability of partner and channel relationships. By defining clear and relevant key performance indicators, setting appropriate targets, and establishing robust monitoring and reporting processes, organisations can gain visibility into what is working well and where improvements are needed. Regularly assessing partner effectiveness and segmenting partners based on value and strategic fit enables targeted management and optimisation of the channel portfolio. Linking performance to rewards and consequences helps to align partner behaviour with business objectives and drive continuous improvement.

However, performance measurement and evaluation should not be viewed as a punitive exercise but rather as an opportunity for growth and collaboration. Sharing best practices, soliciting feedback from partners and customers, and piloting new initiatives are all essential for fostering a culture of innovation and continuous improvement.

Ultimately, the most successful organisations view their channel partners as an extension of their own business and invest in their success accordingly. By taking a data-driven, proactive, and partner-centric approach to performance measurement and evaluation, companies can unlock the full potential of their channel ecosystem and achieve sustainable competitive advantage in an increasingly complex and dynamic business environment.

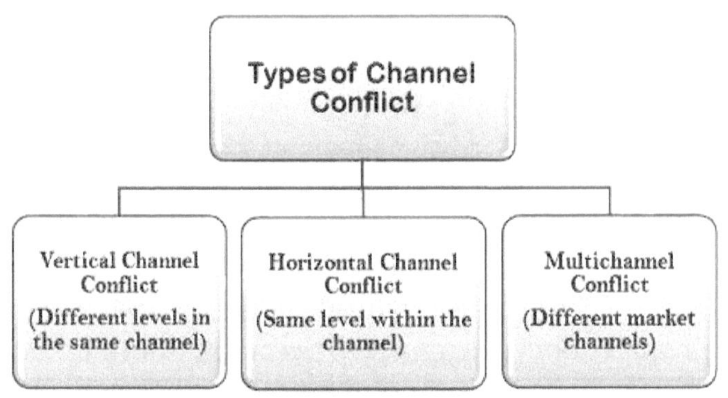

CHAPTER 8

CHANNEL CONFLICT

Introduction to Channel Conflict

In today's highly competitive business landscape, companies increasingly rely on a diverse array of distribution channels to reach their target customers effectively. This multi-channel approach, while offering numerous benefits such as increased market coverage and customer convenience, also gives rise to a growing challenge: channel conflict. Channel conflict refers to the tensions, disputes, and disagreements that can emerge between different members of a company's distribution network, such as manufacturers, wholesalers, retailers, and online platforms. As businesses strive to optimise their channel strategies and maximise their market presence, understanding and effectively managing channel conflict becomes a critical imperative for long-term success. The prevalence of channel conflict has intensified in recent years, driven by several key factors. Firstly, the rapid advancement of digital technologies and e-commerce has disrupted traditional distribution models, enabling companies to bypass intermediaries and sell directly to consumers. This shift has blurred the lines between different channels and created new sources of competition and conflict. Secondly, the increasing sophistication and expectations of customers have pressured companies to provide seamless, omnichannel experiences across multiple touchpoints. Meeting these demands requires close coordination and alignment among channel partners, which can be challenging in the face of divergent goals and priorities. Finally, the globalisation of markets and the emergence of new players have intensified competition and put pressure on margins, leading to heightened tensions and conflicts within distribution networks. Given the significant impact that channel conflict can have on a company's performance, profitability, and customer relationships, it is essential for business leaders to develop a deep understanding of its causes, manifestations, and potential solutions. By proactively addressing the underlying drivers of conflict and fostering a culture of collaboration and mutual benefit among channel partners, companies can mitigate the risks and capitalise on the opportunities presented by a multi-channel distribution strategy. The following pages will delve into the complexities of channel conflict, providing insights and strategies for navigating this critical challenge in today's dynamic business environment.

Understanding the Causes of Channel Conflict

To effectively address and resolve channel conflict, it is crucial to first understand the underlying causes that give rise to these tensions and disputes. While the specific triggers of conflict may vary depending on the industry, market, and channel structure, there are several common factors that contribute to the emergence of channel conflict.

One of the primary causes of channel conflict is the misalignment of goals, incentives, and priorities among different members of the distribution network. Each channel partner, be it a manufacturer, wholesaler, retailer, or online platform, has its own set of objectives, performance metrics, and financial targets. When these goals are not properly aligned or when there is a perceived imbalance in the distribution of benefits and costs, conflicts can arise. For example, a manufacturer may prioritise maintaining a premium brand image and protecting its intellectual property, while a retailer may focus on maximising sales volume and offering competitive prices. These divergent priorities can lead to disputes over pricing strategies, promotional activities, and territory management.

Another significant driver of channel conflict is the lack of clear roles, responsibilities, and communication channels within the distribution network. When there is ambiguity or overlap in the functions and authority of different channel partners, it can create confusion, duplication of efforts, and power struggles. Moreover, the absence of open and transparent communication can exacerbate misunderstandings and fuel mistrust among channel members. Without a clear framework for collaboration and information-sharing, channel partners may operate in silos, leading to inconsistencies in customer experiences and erosion of brand value.

The rapid evolution of technology and changes in consumer behaviour also contribute to the emergence of channel conflict. The rise of e-commerce and direct-to-consumer models has disrupted traditional distribution channels, creating new sources of competition and blurring the lines between different channels. As customers increasingly expect seamless, omnichannel experiences, companies must navigate the complexities of integrating online and offline channels while ensuring consistency in pricing, promotions, and customer service. This omnichannel imperative can strain relationships among channel partners, particularly when there is a perception of favouritism or inequitable treatment.

Furthermore, the globalisation of markets and the entry of new players can intensify competition and put pressure on margins, leading to heightened tensions within distribution networks. As companies expand into new geographies and face local competitors, they may need to adapt their channel strategies and pricing models to remain competitive. This can create conflicts with existing channel partners who may feel threatened or disadvantaged by these changes. Additionally, the emergence of disruptive business models, such as subscription services or sharing economies, can challenge traditional channel structures and create new sources of conflict.

Understanding these underlying causes of channel conflict is essential for developing effective strategies to prevent, mitigate, and resolve disputes. By recognising the diverse goals, priorities, and challenges faced by different channel partners, companies can proactively address potential sources of tension and foster a culture of collaboration and mutual benefit. This requires open communication, clear roles and responsibilities, and a commitment to aligning incentives and rewards across the distribution network. Moreover, by staying attuned to the evolving technological and competitive landscape, companies can adapt their channel strategies to minimise conflicts and capitalise on emerging opportunities. The following pages will explore the manifestations of channel conflict and their impact on business performance, as well as provide practical strategies for managing and resolving these challenges.

Manifestations of Channel Conflict

Channel conflict can manifest in various forms, each presenting unique challenges and implications for businesses operating in complex distribution networks. These manifestations can range from minor disagreements and tensions to full-blown disputes and legal battles, depending on the severity and duration of the conflict. Understanding the different types of channel conflict is crucial for developing targeted strategies to address and resolve these issues effectively.

One common manifestation of channel conflict is price competition, which occurs when different channel partners offer the same products or services at varying prices. This can lead to price wars, margin erosion, and customer confusion, as well as undermine the perceived value and consistency of the brand. Price competition can arise due to a lack of clear pricing policies, disparities in cost structures, or the presence of grey markets where products are sold through unauthorised channels. To mitigate price competition, companies need to establish and enforce clear pricing guidelines, monitor market prices regularly, and ensure that all channel partners have access to fair and competitive terms.

Another manifestation of channel conflict is territory encroachment, which happens when one channel partner enters or expands into a geographic area or customer segment that is already served by another partner. This can create direct competition, erode market share, and strain relationships among channel members. Territory encroachment can be particularly challenging in contexts where exclusive distribution rights have been granted or where there are significant differences in market maturity or customer preferences across regions. To prevent and address territory encroachment, companies should establish clear and enforceable territory boundaries, provide incentives for channel partners to respect these boundaries and have mechanisms in place to quickly detect and resolve any violations.

Channel conflict can also manifest in the form of brand inconsistency, which arises when different channel partners present conflicting or inconsistent messages, images, or experiences to customers. This can dilute brand equity, create customer confusion, and undermine trust in the brand. Brand inconsistency can occur due to a lack of clear brand guidelines, insufficient training and support for channel partners, or the presence of counterfeit or grey market products. To maintain brand consistency, companies need to develop and communicate clear brand standards, provide regular training and resources to channel partners and monitor and enforce compliance with brand guidelines across all channels.

A fourth manifestation of channel conflict is the misallocation of resources and support, which happens when there is an uneven or unfair distribution of marketing, training, or financial support among channel partners. This can create resentment, demotivate channel partners, and hinder the overall performance of the distribution network. Misallocation of resources can arise due to favouritism, historical biases, or a lack of transparency in decision-making processes. To ensure fair and effective allocation of resources, companies should establish clear and objective criteria for resource allocation, involve channel partners in planning and budgeting processes, and regularly review and adjust support levels based on performance and market feedback.

Finally, channel conflict can manifest in the form of power imbalances and trust issues, which occur when there are significant differences in bargaining power, information access, or perceived value among channel partners. This can lead to one-sided negotiations, opportunistic behaviour, and a breakdown of trust and collaboration within the distribution network. Power imbalances can be particularly acute in contexts where there are a few dominant players or where there is a high degree of dependence on a single channel partner. To address power imbalances and build trust, companies need to foster open and transparent communication, create opportunities for joint problem-solving and value creation, and establish fair and mutually beneficial contracts and performance metrics.

Recognising and understanding these different manifestations of channel conflict is essential for developing a comprehensive and proactive approach to conflict management. By identifying the specific types of conflict that are most prevalent or impactful in their distribution networks, companies can prioritise their efforts and resources accordingly. Moreover, by addressing the root causes of conflict and implementing targeted strategies to prevent and resolve disputes, businesses can create a more collaborative, efficient, and profitable distribution ecosystem. The next page will explore the impact of channel conflict on business performance and highlight the importance of effective conflict management for long-term success.

Impact of Channel Conflict on Business Performance

Channel conflict can have far-reaching and detrimental effects on a company's business performance, affecting various aspects of its operations, profitability, and customer relationships. Left unchecked, channel conflict can erode the value and competitiveness of a company's offerings, damage its reputation, and hinder its ability to achieve its strategic goals. Understanding the multifaceted impact of channel conflict is crucial for building a compelling case for proactive conflict management and securing the necessary resources and support to address these challenges effectively.

One of the most direct and visible impacts of channel conflict is on sales and market share. When channel partners engage in price wars, territory encroachment, or brand inconsistency, it can lead to a decline in sales volume, revenue, and profitability. Customers may become confused or frustrated by conflicting offers or experiences, leading them to delay or abandon their purchases. Moreover, the presence of unauthorised or grey market channels can divert sales away from legitimate partners, eroding their incentives to invest in the brand and support its growth. Over time, these dynamics can result in a loss of market share to competitors who are able to provide a more consistent and compelling value proposition to customers.

Channel conflict can also have a significant impact on a company's cost structure and operational efficiency. When channel partners engage in duplicative or conflicting activities, such as overlapping marketing campaigns or redundant inventory management, it can lead to wasted resources and increased costs. Moreover, the time and effort required to manage and resolve channel conflicts can divert attention and resources away from more productive and value-adding activities, such as innovation, customer service, and market development. In some cases, channel conflict can even lead to legal disputes or regulatory investigations, which can be costly and time-consuming to resolve.

Another key impact of channel conflict is on customer satisfaction and loyalty. When customers experience inconsistent or conflicting messages, prices, or experiences across different channels, it can undermine their trust and confidence in the brand. Moreover, if channel partners engage in behaviour that is perceived as unfair or unethical, such as price gouging or bait-and-switch tactics, it can damage the company's reputation and alienate customers. Over time, these negative experiences can lead to a decline in customer loyalty, advocacy, and lifetime value as customers choose to take their business elsewhere.

Channel conflict can also have a negative impact on the motivation and performance of channel partners themselves. When partners feel that they are being treated unfairly or that their interests are not being adequately considered, it can lead to resentment, disengagement, and even active sabotage. Moreover, if partners perceive that the company is not providing sufficient support or resources to help them succeed, they may choose to focus their efforts on other brands or opportunities that offer a better return on investment. This can lead to a vicious cycle of declining performance and increasing conflict, which can be difficult to break without a concerted effort to rebuild trust and alignment. Finally, channel conflict can have a broader impact on a company's ability to achieve its strategic goals and adapt to changing market conditions. When channel partners are not aligned around a common vision and strategy, it can hinder the company's ability to execute its plans effectively and respond to new opportunities or threats. Moreover, if channel conflict is allowed to persist or escalate, it can damage the company's relationships with key stakeholders, such as suppliers, investors, and regulators, making it more difficult to secure the resources and support needed to drive long-term growth and success.

Given the significant and multifaceted impact of channel conflict on business performance, it is essential for companies to prioritise conflict management as a key strategic imperative. By investing in the necessary processes, tools, and capabilities to prevent, detect, and resolve conflicts effectively, companies can create a more collaborative, efficient, and profitable distribution ecosystem. This requires a proactive and holistic approach that addresses the root causes of conflict, aligns incentives and rewards, and fosters a culture of trust and mutual benefit among all channel partners. The next page will explore some specific strategies and best practices for managing channel conflict effectively.

Strategies for Managing Channel Conflict

Effectively managing channel conflict requires a multifaceted and proactive approach that addresses the underlying causes of conflict, aligns incentives and goals, and fosters a culture of collaboration and mutual benefit among all channel partners. While the specific strategies and tactics may vary depending on the industry, market, and channel structure, there are several key principles and best practices that can guide companies in developing a comprehensive and effective conflict management programme.

1. Establish clear and consistent policies and guidelines

One of the most important steps in managing channel conflict is to establish clear and consistent policies and guidelines that govern all aspects of the distribution network, including pricing, territory management, brand standards, and partner support. These policies should be based on a thorough understanding of the market dynamics, customer needs, and competitive landscape and should be designed to promote fair and equitable treatment of all channel partners. Moreover, these policies should be communicated clearly and consistently to all partners and should be enforced fairly and transparently to ensure compliance and maintain trust.

2. Foster open and transparent communication

Effective communication is essential for preventing and resolving channel conflicts. Companies should establish regular and open channels of communication with all channel partners, including face-to-face meetings, conference calls, and online forums, to share information, gather feedback, and address concerns. Moreover, companies should be transparent about their goals, strategies, and performance metrics and should involve channel partners in key decision-making processes to build trust and alignment. By fostering a culture of open and honest communication, companies can identify potential conflicts early on and work collaboratively to find mutually beneficial solutions.

3. Align incentives and rewards

Another key strategy for managing channel conflict is to align incentives and rewards across all channel partners. This means designing compensation and incentive programmes that encourage desired behaviours and outcomes, such as customer satisfaction, brand loyalty, and revenue growth, while discouraging undesirable behaviours, such as price discounting or territory encroachment. Moreover, incentives should be structured in a way that promotes collaboration and mutual benefit rather than competition and zero-sum thinking. For example, companies can offer joint marketing funds, co-op advertising programmes, or volume-based rebates that reward partners for working together to grow the overall market.

4. Provide training and support

Effective conflict management also requires providing channel partners with the necessary training, tools, and support to succeed in their roles. This includes product and sales training, marketing and promotional support, and technical and customer service assistance.

By investing in the development and empowerment of channel partners, companies can help them to better serve customers, represent the brand, and achieve their performance goals. Moreover, by providing a consistent and high-quality level of support across all channels, companies can ensure a more seamless and satisfying customer experience, which can help to prevent conflicts and build loyalty.

5. Monitor and measure performance

To effectively manage channel conflict, companies must also have robust systems and processes in place to monitor and measure the performance of all channel partners. This includes tracking key metrics such as sales volume, market share, customer satisfaction, and partner engagement and using this data to identify trends, gaps, and opportunities for improvement. Moreover, companies should establish clear and objective criteria for evaluating partner performance and should use this information to make data-driven decisions about resource allocation, incentives, and support. By continuously monitoring and optimising channel performance, companies can proactively identify and address potential conflicts before they escalate.

6. Establish a conflict resolution process

Despite best efforts to prevent and manage conflicts, disputes and disagreements are likely to arise from time to time in any distribution network. Therefore, it is essential to have a clear and effective process in place for resolving conflicts when they do occur. This process should involve a neutral and impartial third-party, such as a mediator or arbitrator, who can help the parties identify the underlying issues, explore options, and reach a mutually acceptable resolution. Moreover, the process should be designed to promote open and constructive dialogue rather than adversarial or punitive actions and should focus on finding win-win solutions that benefit all parties involved.

7. Foster a culture of collaboration and continuous improvement

Finally, effective channel conflict management requires fostering a culture of collaboration, innovation, and continuous improvement across the entire distribution network. This means encouraging all channel partners to share ideas, best practices, and feedback and to work together to identify and pursue new opportunities for growth and value creation. Moreover, it means creating an environment where experimentation, learning, and adaptation are valued and rewarded and where conflicts are viewed as opportunities for improvement rather than sources of blame or punishment. By cultivating a culture of collaboration and continuous improvement, companies can create a more agile, resilient, and successful distribution ecosystem that can weather the challenges and seize the opportunities of an ever-changing market. Managing channel conflict is a complex and ongoing process that requires a strategic, proactive, and collaborative approach. By establishing clear policies and guidelines, fostering open communication, aligning incentives and rewards, providing training and support, monitoring and measuring performance, establishing a conflict resolution process, and fostering a culture of collaboration and continuous improvement, companies can effectively prevent, detect, and resolve conflicts in their distribution networks. Moreover, by viewing conflict management as a key driver of business performance and customer value rather than a necessary evil or cost of doing business, companies can create a more sustainable and profitable distribution ecosystem that benefits all stakeholders involved.

CHAPTER 9

STRATEGIC ALLIANCES AND PARTNERSHIPS

Importance of Strategic Alliances

As a consequence of strategic alliances, companies are also able to mitigate risks and overcome obstacles that may be insurmountable when operating independently.

Having strategic alliances also gives companies the opportunity to mitigate risks and overcome barriers that may otherwise be insurmountable if they operate independently.

Furthermore, strategic alliances allow companies to mitigate risks as well as overcome barriers that they might find insurmountable in their independent operations as a result of a strategic alliance.

Moreover, strategic alliances also provide companies with the ability to mitigate risks and overcome barriers that may seem insurmountable when operating independently in a competitive environment.

A strategic alliance can help companies mitigate risks and overcome barriers that may be insurmountable for independent companies if they operate independently, as strategic alliances enable them to do.

As well as this, it is important to point out that strategic alliances also enable companies to mitigate risks and to overcome barriers that may be difficult to overcome for them if they operate alone.

It is also worth mentioning that strategic alliances can, in fact, be a very useful tool for companies, allowing them to mitigate risks and overcome barriers that otherwise might not be possible if they operated alone.

It is also important to keep in mind that strategic alliances are important for companies, as they allow them to mitigate risks and overcome barriers that might otherwise be impossible for them when operating alone.

Importance of Strategic Alliances (Continued)

In the current highly competitive business environment, it is impossible to overstate the importance of strategic alliances in achieving business success.

As a whole, strategic alliances cannot be overstated in the highly competitive business environment in which we live today.

As a result, it cannot be stressed enough that strategic alliances have become increasingly important when it comes to today's highly competitive business environment.

Regardless of the specific nature of the alliance, it cannot be overstated that the importance of strategic alliances cannot be overstated in these highly competitive times.

Overall, it is important to remember the importance of strategic alliances in today's highly competitive business environment because it cannot be overstated.

It cannot be overstated how important strategic alliances are in the modern business environment, as it has become increasingly difficult to compete among the major players.

The importance of strategic alliances in today's highly competitive business environment cannot be overstated in terms of its importance in terms of the performance of firms.

A strategic alliance is an invaluable tool for businesses in today's highly competitive marketplace. It cannot be overemphasised how important it is.

It must be acknowledged that the importance of strategic alliances cannot be overstated in today's highly competitive business environment where business is highly competitive.

It cannot be overstated that strategic alliances are crucial for today's highly competitive business environment.

Types of Channel Partnerships

The distribution partnership is one of the most common types of channel partnerships. In this type of partnership, companies collaborate to distribute products and services through shared channels or networks in order to reach a wider audience.

A common type of channel partnership is distribution partnerships, which involve the collaboration of companies to distribute their products or services through a network or channel shared by both companies. There are several different types of channel partnerships, but a common one is distribution partnerships, in which companies collaborate with each other to market products or services via shared channels or networks.

As a result of channel partnerships, there are many types of agreements that companies can enter into, such as distribution agreements, in which companies collaborate and share channels or networks to distribute products and services. A common type of channel partnership is a distribution partnership, which involves companies collaborating to distribute goods or services through a common channel or network that they both operate.

Distribution partnerships are the most common type of channel partnership, where companies collaborate to distribute products or services to customers through a network of shared channels or distribution networks. There are different types of channel partnerships, but distribution partnerships can be considered to be the most common. In distribution partnerships, companies cooperate to distribute products or services using shared channels or networks.

One of the most common types of channel partnerships is distribution partnerships, where companies collaborate to sell their products or services through channels and networks that they share. A common type of channel partnership is a distribution partnership, where the companies collaborate to deliver products or services through a shared channel or network on a wide scale.

Types of Channel Partnerships (Continued)

A number of other types of channel partnerships exist, including co-promotions, where companies collaborate on promotional campaigns or events, and joint ventures, where companies establish a separate legal entity to pursue a specific business opportunity.

As an alternative to channel partnerships, there are other types of partnerships, such as co-promotions, where companies work together on promotional campaigns and events, as well as joint ventures, where organisations form a separate legal entity in order to pursue a specific business opportunity.

Co-promotions are another type of channel partnership. These include collaborations between companies on promotional campaigns, events, and joint ventures, in which companies form a separate legal entity to pursue a specific business opportunity.

The other types of channel partnerships include co-promotions, where companies collaborate on promotional campaigns or events, and joint ventures, where companies form their own legal entities to pursue a particular business opportunity or to follow a specific marketing plan.

Building and Managing Strategic Alliances

As soon as the partners have been identified, the next step would be to negotiate the terms of the alliance agreement, which would include roles, responsibilities, resource allocation, and governance structures.

As soon as partners are identified, the next step is to negotiate the terms of the alliance agreement, which includes roles, responsibilities, the allocation of resources and the governance structure of the alliance.

Following the identification of the alliance partners, the next step will be to negotiate the terms of the alliance agreement, which includes the roles, responsibilities, resource allocation, and governance structures of the alliance.

Upon the identification of partners, the next step is to negotiate the terms and conditions of the alliance agreement, including the roles and responsibilities, resource allocation, governance structures, and resource allocation processes.

A partnership agreement is negotiated once the partners have been identified, and the terms of the agreement include the roles of each party, their responsibilities, and how resources will be allocated and how governance will be distributed.

After identifying potential partners for the alliance, the next step will be to negotiate the terms of the alliance agreement, including the roles, responsibilities, resource allocation, and governance structures that will govern the alliance in the future.

It is the next step after you have identified the alliance partners that you will need to negotiate the terms of the alliance agreement, including roles, responsibilities, asset allocations, governance structures, and resource allocations within the alliance.

Building and Managing Strategic Alliances (Continued)

In order to facilitate communication, resolve conflicts, and address any issues or challenges that are likely to arise in the course of a partnership, alliance managers play a critical role.

Alliance managers play a key role in facilitating communication within the organisation, resolving conflicts that may arise between the partners, and addressing any issues or challenges that may arise during the partnership.

Managers of alliances play a very important role in facilitating communication, resolving conflicts, and handling issues that may arise during the partnership period, as well as addressing any challenges that could arise.

A key aspect of alliance management is facilitating communication among the partners, resolving conflicts, and dealing with any issues or challenges that may arise during the partnership's development.

As part of the management of an alliance, it is essential to facilitate communication, resolve conflicts, and identify and address any issues or challenges that may arise during the course of the partnership.

It is the alliance managers' role to facilitate communication in the partnership, resolve conflicts, and deal with any issues or challenges that may arise during the relationships that may arise during the partnership period.

As a member of an alliance management team, one of the main responsibilities of this role is to encourage communication, resolve conflict, and address any issues or challenges that may arise during the partnership.

Managers of alliances play a crucial role in facilitating communication, resolving conflict, and addressing any issues or challenges that may arise during the partnership and extend the lifetime of the partnership.

In order to facilitate communication, to resolve conflicts, and to address any issues or challenges that may arise during a partnership, alliance managers play a very important part.

Collaborative Innovation and Value Creation

When partners work together to identify market opportunities, develop new technologies, or solve complex problems, collaborative innovation occurs as a result of their collaboration.

As a result of collaborative innovation, partners are able to identify new market opportunities, develop new technologies, or solve complex problems by working together.

The concept of collaborative innovation refers to how partners work together to identify market opportunities, develop new technologies, or solve complex problems in a collaborative manner.

In the process of collaboration innovation, partners come together in order to identify market opportunities, develop new technologies, or find solutions to complex problems.

In the case of collaborative innovation, two or more companies work together to identify and develop new market opportunities as well as solve complex problems by developing new technologies.

In order for collaborative innovation to take place, partners have to work together to identify market opportunities, develop new technologies, or solve complex problems that occur in the world.

In collaboration innovation, partners use their combined skills and abilities to identify market opportunities, develop new technologies, and solve complex problems together.

When partners come together to identify market opportunities, develop new technologies, or solve complex problems together, then it will be called collaborative innovation.

Collaborative Innovation and Value Creation (Continued)

The importance of collaborative innovation lies in the fact that it can often lead to the creation of unique value propositions that differentiate partners in the marketplace. Moreover, collaborative innovation often leads to the creation of unique value propositions that allow partners to differentiate themselves from the competition in the marketplace.

It is also important to note that, as a result of collaborative innovation, it is not uncommon for partners to market unique value propositions that differentiate them from each other. Also, collaborative innovation often leads to a unique value proposition that distinguishes partners in the marketplace based on their unique contribution to it.

It should be noted that collaborative innovation often results in unique value propositions being created, which help differentiate partners in the market Additionally, collaborative innovation leads to the creation of unique value propositions that differentiate partners in the marketplace as a result of their unique collaboration.

Additionally, collaborative innovation leads to the creation of unique value propositions that differentiate partners in the marketplace as a result of their unique collaboration. It is important to realise that collaboration can lead to the creation of unique value propositions that can differentiate partners in the marketplace from one another.

Moreover, collaborative innovation often leads to the creation of unique value propositions that enable partners to compete in the market on the basis of their competitive advantages. In addition, collaborative innovation often results in unique value propositions that contribute to the differentiation of partners in the market and contribute to their success.

Moreover, collaborative innovation can often result in the development of unique value propositions that differentiate companies within a market and help differentiate partners from competitors.

Case Studies and Practical Insights

Real-world case studies provide valuable insights into successful strategic alliances and partnerships in various industries. These case studies offer concrete examples of how companies have leveraged alliances to achieve specific business objectives, drive growth, and create value for their stakeholders.

By examining the strategies, challenges, and outcomes of these alliances, companies can glean practical insights and lessons learned that can inform their own partnership strategies. Key success factors, best practices, and potential pitfalls are highlighted, providing valuable guidance for companies embarking on their alliance journey.

Case studies also showcase the diversity of strategic alliances and partnerships, illustrating how companies across different industries and regions have successfully collaborated to achieve mutual goals. From distribution partnerships and marketing alliances to joint ventures and strategic alliances, the case studies offer a comprehensive overview of the various forms and applications of channel partnerships.

By studying these real-world examples, companies can gain a deeper understanding of the potential benefits and challenges of strategic alliances and identify opportunities for partnerships that align with their own strategic objectives and priorities.

Case Study 1: Starbucks and Nestlé

In 2018, Starbucks and Nestlé announced a global coffee alliance whereby Nestlé acquired the rights to market, sell, and distribute Starbucks' packaged coffee and tea products globally. This strategic partnership combined Nestlé's vast distribution network and marketing expertise with Starbucks' iconic brand and premium coffee offerings.

Key Success Factors:

Market Expansion: Nestlé gained access to Starbucks' extensive portfolio of premium coffee products, allowing it to expand its presence in the high-growth coffee segment.

Distribution Synergies: Nestlé leveraged its global distribution network to increase the availability of Starbucks products in supermarkets, convenience stores, and online channels worldwide.

Brand Collaboration: The partnership leveraged the strengths of both brands, with Starbucks benefiting from Nestlé's marketing prowess while retaining control over its brand image and product quality.

Challenges and Lessons Learned:

Brand Protection: Starbucks had to ensure that its brand integrity and quality standards were maintained throughout the distribution process, requiring close collaboration with Nestlé to align product standards and marketing strategies.

Market Competition: The partnership faced competition from established coffee brands and private-label offerings, requiring continuous innovation and differentiation to maintain market share and drive growth.

Customer Engagement: Both companies focused on engaging customers through targeted marketing campaigns, product innovations, and experiential initiatives to drive brand loyalty and market penetration.

Case Study 2: Apple and Nike

Apple and Nike collaborated on the development of the Nike+iPod Sport Kit, a wireless system that allowed Nike shoes to communicate with iPods to track running performance. This strategic alliance leveraged Apple's expertise in technology and design with Nike's brand strength and expertise in sports and fitness.

Key Success Factors:

Product Innovation: The Nike+iPod Sport Kit combined Nike's expertise in athletic footwear and apparel with Apple's cutting-edge technology, resulting in a groundbreaking product that revolutionised the fitness tracking industry.

Brand Integration: The partnership seamlessly integrated Nike's branding and design aesthetics with Apple's user-friendly interface and ecosystem, creating a cohesive and compelling user experience.

Market Expansion: The collaboration allowed both companies to tap into new customer segments and markets, as the product appealed to both Nike's loyal customer base and Apple's tech-savvy customers.

Challenges and Lessons Learned:

Technical Integration: Developing a seamless and reliable wireless communication system between Nike shoes and Apple devices required extensive research, development, and testing to ensure compatibility and performance.

Data Privacy and Security: Both companies had to address concerns related to data privacy and security, particularly regarding the collection and use of personal health and fitness data by the Nike+iPod Sport Kit.

Market Adoption: While the product received positive reviews from critics and customers, market adoption initially faced challenges related to pricing, compatibility, and customer education. However, ongoing marketing efforts and product iterations helped drive adoption and market penetration over time.

These case studies demonstrate the power of strategic alliances and partnerships in driving innovation, expanding market reach, and creating value for both companies and customers. By leveraging each other's strengths and resources, companies can achieve mutual goals and unlock new growth opportunities in today's competitive marketplace.

Conclusion

In conclusion, strategic alliances and partnerships play a vital role in channel management, enabling companies to access new markets, drive innovation, and create value for their stakeholders. By forging collaborative relationships with complementary partners, companies can leverage shared resources, expertise, and networks to achieve mutual goals and capitalise on market opportunities.

Effective alliance development and management require careful planning, clear communication, and mutual trust. By following best practices and learning from real-world case studies, companies can maximise the benefits of strategic alliances and position themselves for sustained success in today's competitive marketplace.

As companies continue to navigate an increasingly complex and dynamic business environment, strategic alliances will remain a cornerstone of effective channel management. By embracing collaboration, fostering innovation, and building strong partnerships, companies can enhance their competitiveness, drive growth, and create long-term value for their customers, partners, and shareholders.

CHAPTER 10

RESILIENCE IN CHANNEL MANAGEMENT

Introduction to Resilience in Channel Management

In an era marked by unprecedented disruptions and rapid changes, resilience within distribution channels stands as a cornerstone for businesses aiming to thrive amidst uncertainties. This section delves into the essence of resilience within channel management, highlighting its profound significance in maintaining operational continuity, adapting to disruptions, and driving sustainable growth.

Amidst the complexities of today's business landscape, characterised by geopolitical tensions, supply chain disruptions, technological advancements, and shifting customer preferences, resilience emerges as a critical capability that separates successful organisations from those that falter. Resilience within channel management involves cultivating a robust and agile network of partners, suppliers, and distribution channels, capable of withstanding shocks and pivoting swiftly in response to evolving market dynamics.

Resilience goes beyond mere survival; it embodies the ability to anticipate risks proactively, adapt to changing circumstances with alacrity, and foster innovation amid uncertainties. By fostering resilience, businesses can mitigate the impact of disruptions, seize emerging opportunities, and maintain a competitive edge in turbulent times. This chapter aims to dissect the core principles, strategies, and practices that underpin resilience in channel management, equipping businesses with the tools and insights needed to navigate through turbulent times successfully.

Building resilience within distribution channels necessitates a multifaceted approach, encompassing risk assessment, diversification, agility, and collaborative partnerships. Organisations must conduct comprehensive risk assessments to identify potential vulnerabilities within their supply chains, distribution networks, and partner ecosystems. By understanding these risks, businesses can proactively develop contingency plans, implement mitigation strategies, and allocate resources effectively to bolster resilience.

Moreover, diversification plays a pivotal role in enhancing resilience. By diversifying sources of supply, distribution channels, and market reach, organisations can reduce their reliance on single points of failure and minimise the impact of localised disruptions. This approach fosters redundancy and provides alternative pathways for maintaining business continuity in the face of adverse events.

Agility, the ability to respond swiftly to changing circumstances, is another cornerstone of resilience within channel management. Agile organisations can rapidly reconfigure their distribution networks, reallocate resources, and adapt their strategies to align with evolving market conditions. Fostering a culture of continuous improvement, embracing digital transformation, and leveraging data-driven insights are crucial enablers of agility, empowering businesses to make informed decisions and execute course corrections promptly.

Furthermore, resilience thrives on collaborative partnerships and stakeholder engagement. By fostering strong relationships with suppliers, logistics providers, and distribution partners, organisations can collectively navigate challenges, share best practices, and leverage collective resources. Effective communication, transparency, and trust are vital elements of these collaborative efforts, ensuring seamless coordination and synchronised responses to disruptions.

In this chapter, we will explore the multifaceted dimensions of resilience within channel management, delving into real-world case studies, practical strategies, and actionable insights. By embracing resilience as a core organisational capability, businesses can fortify their distribution channels, mitigate risks, and position themselves for long-term success in an ever-changing and unpredictable global marketplace.

Building Resilient Distribution Channels

Diversification: Diversifying distribution channels involves expanding the portfolio of channels through which products or services are delivered to customers. This approach helps mitigate risks by reducing overreliance on any single channel. Companies can explore new geographic markets, leverage diverse sales channels (e.g., brick-and-mortar, e-commerce, direct-to-customer), and target niche customer segments. Diversification also extends to the supply chain, where companies can source materials and components from multiple suppliers, reducing the impact of disruptions affecting any single vendor. By distributing risk across multiple channels and suppliers, companies can maintain operational continuity and revenue streams even if one channel or supplier experiences disruptions.

Redundancy: Closely linked to diversification, redundancy involves establishing backup systems, alternative supply sources, and contingency plans. This redundancy can take various forms, such as maintaining safety stock levels, having multiple production facilities in different regions, or contracting with secondary suppliers. Redundancy acts as a safeguard, ensuring that critical components, materials, or finished goods can be sourced from alternative sources if the primary channel is disrupted. It provides a buffer against potential shocks and enables businesses to switch to alternative channels or suppliers seamlessly, minimising downtime and ensuring uninterrupted operations.

Agility: In an ever-changing business landscape, agility is crucial for adapting to shifts in demand, customer preferences, and market conditions. Agile distribution channels can rapidly scale-up or down, adjust inventory levels, and reconfigure logistics networks in response to evolving needs. This agility requires end-to-end visibility across the supply chain, enabling real-time monitoring and decision-making. Leveraging advanced technologies, such as predictive analytics, real-time tracking, and flexible fulfilment solutions, can enhance agility and responsiveness within distribution channels. Additionally, fostering a culture of continuous improvement and empowering frontline employees to make decisions can further contribute to organisational agility.

Collaboration: Building resilient distribution channels is a collaborative effort that involves stakeholders across the entire value chain. Effective collaboration with suppliers, logistics providers, channel partners, and even competitors can yield significant benefits. Information-sharing, joint planning, and coordinated responses to disruptions can help minimise supply chain risks and ensure continuity of operations. Collaborative partnerships may involve sharing resources, co-investing in infrastructure, or establishing joint contingency plans. Strong communication, trust, and aligned incentives are essential for successful collaboration, enabling stakeholders to work together towards common goals and respond collectively to challenges.

By strategically combining diversification, redundancy, agility, and collaboration, companies can create a robust and resilient distribution network capable of withstanding disruptions, adapting to change, and seizing new opportunities. This multifaceted approach not only enhances risk management but also fosters innovation, customer satisfaction, and long-term competitive advantage in an increasingly volatile and uncertain business environment.

Resilience Planning and Preparedness

Risk Assessment: Risk assessment is a crucial first step in building resilient distribution channels. It involves identifying and evaluating potential risks and vulnerabilities across the entire distribution network, including suppliers, transportation, warehousing, and last-mile delivery. By conducting comprehensive risk assessments, companies can gain insights into the nature and magnitude of risks, enabling them to develop targeted strategies to mitigate, transfer, or accept risks based on their tolerance levels and business objectives.

Risk assessment typically involves a structured process of risk identification, analysis, and evaluation. Companies may leverage tools such as risk registers, value chain mapping, and scenario analysis to identify potential risks systematically. These risks can range from supply chain disruptions, natural disasters, cyber threats, geopolitical tensions, regulatory changes, and shifts in customer demand.

Once risks are identified, companies can analyse their likelihood of occurrence and potential impact on distribution channels, operations, and financial performance. This analysis enables organisations to prioritise risks based on their severity and develop appropriate risk mitigation strategies.

Effective risk assessment requires collaboration across various departments, including supply chain, operations, finance, and risk management. It also involves engaging with external stakeholders, such as suppliers, logistics providers, and industry experts, to gather diverse perspectives and leverage collective knowledge.

Resilience Planning and Preparedness (Continued)

Scenario Planning: Complementing risk assessment, scenario planning is a proactive approach that helps organisations prepare for and respond to disruptions effectively. By simulating plausible scenarios and assessing their potential impact on distribution channels, companies can identify critical vulnerabilities, develop response strategies, and enhance their preparedness for unforeseen events.

Scenario planning involves creating hypothetical yet realistic scenarios based on identified risks, industry trends, and market dynamics. These scenarios may include supply chain disruptions, natural disasters, cyber-attacks, economic downturns, or regulatory changes. For each scenario, organisations can analyse the potential consequences on their distribution channels, such as disruptions in supply, transportation challenges, inventory shortages, or changes in customer demand.

Through scenario planning, companies can develop contingency plans and response strategies tailored to each scenario. These plans may include alternative sourcing strategies, inventory management approaches, logistics rerouting, and communication protocols. By exploring various scenarios, organisations can identify potential bottlenecks, resource constraints, and capacity limitations, enabling them to proactively address these issues and enhance their resilience.

Scenario planning encourages cross-functional collaboration and facilitates strategic discussions among stakeholders, fostering a shared understanding of risks and preparedness measures. It also promotes a culture of continuous improvement by regularly reviewing and updating scenarios based on changing market conditions and emerging risks.

Resilience Planning and Preparedness (Continued)

Crisis Management: Effective crisis management is essential for mitigating the impact of disruptions and ensuring business continuity. It involves establishing robust protocols and response mechanisms to manage disruptions effectively, enabling companies to coordinate response efforts, communicate transparently with stakeholders, and minimise the impact on distribution channels and business operations.

Crisis management planning typically involves several key components:

1. **Crisis Response Team**: Establishing a dedicated crisis response team with clearly defined roles and responsibilities is crucial. This team should comprise cross-functional experts from various departments, such as supply chain, operations, risk management, legal, and communications.

2. **Communication Protocols**: Developing clear communication protocols is vital for ensuring timely and transparent communication with internal and external stakeholders during a crisis. This includes identifying communication channels, spokespersons, and processes for disseminating information to employees, customers, suppliers, and other relevant parties.

3. **Incident Response Plans**: Comprehensive incident response plans should be developed to address specific types of disruptions, such as natural disasters, cyber incidents, or supplier

failures. These plans should outline step-by-step actions to be taken, resource allocation, and decision-making processes to minimise the impact and restore normal operations as quickly as possible.

4. **Business Continuity Planning:** Business continuity planning ensures that critical business functions and distribution channels can continue operating during and after a crisis. This may involve identifying alternative suppliers, transportation routes, or distribution facilities, as well as implementing remote work arrangements and technology solutions to maintain operations.

5. **Training and Simulations:** Regular training and crisis simulations are essential for ensuring that the crisis management team and relevant stakeholders are prepared to respond effectively. These exercises help identify gaps, test response protocols, and refine crisis management plans based on real-world scenarios.

6. **Post-Crisis Review**: After a crisis, conducting a thorough review and debriefing is crucial for identifying lessons learned, evaluating the effectiveness of the response, and implementing improvements to enhance future preparedness.

Effective crisis management requires a proactive mindset, cross-functional collaboration, and a culture of continuous improvement. By implementing robust crisis management protocols, companies can minimise the impact of disruptions, maintain operational continuity, and protect their reputation and stakeholder trust during challenging times.

Technology and Innovation for Resilient Distribution Channels

Technology and innovation play a pivotal role in enhancing the resilience of distribution channels, empowering companies to enhance visibility, agility, and responsiveness. This section explores key technologies and innovative practices for building resilience within distribution channels.

Supply Chain Visibility: Enhanced supply chain visibility is a critical enabler of resilience in distribution channels. By leveraging technologies such as Internet of Things (IoT) sensors, radio-frequency identification (RFID) tags, and blockchain, companies can gain real-time visibility into the movement of goods, inventory levels, and the status of shipments across the entire supply chain. This end-to-end visibility enables proactive monitoring and identification of potential disruptions, allowing companies to respond swiftly and mitigate the impact on their distribution channels.

IoT sensors and RFID tags provide granular tracking data, enabling companies to monitor environmental conditions, identify delays, and detect anomalies in real-time. Blockchain technology, with its decentralised and immutable ledger, offers transparency and traceability, ensuring the integrity of data shared among supply chain partners. By integrating these technologies, companies can gain a comprehensive view of their distribution channels, identify bottlenecks, optimise routes, and make informed decisions to maintain operational continuity during disruptions.

Technology and Innovation for Resilient Distribution Channels (Continued)

Predictive Analytics: Predictive analytics leverages advanced algorithms, machine learning, and big data to anticipate changes in market demand, identify emerging trends, and forecast potential disruptions. By analysing historical data, market trends, customer behaviour, and external factors, companies can develop sophisticated predictive models that provide valuable insights into future scenarios.

These predictive models can forecast demand patterns, identify potential supply chain risks, and optimise inventory levels across distribution channels. By anticipating changes in demand or potential disruptions, companies can proactively adjust their distribution strategies, reallocate resources, and implement contingency plans, minimising the impact on operations and customer satisfaction.

Furthermore, predictive analytics can support risk assessment and scenario planning by simulating various scenarios and quantifying their potential impact on distribution channels. This enables companies to prioritise risks, develop targeted mitigation strategies, and enhance their overall preparedness for disruptions.

Technology and Innovation for Resilient Distribution Channels (Continued)

Cloud Computing Cloud computing offers scalability, flexibility, and resilience, enabling companies to build agile and adaptable distribution channels. By leveraging cloud-based solutions for supply chain management, companies can streamline collaboration, automate processes, and enhance scalability, ensuring operational continuity even in adverse conditions.

Cloud-based platforms provide a centralised hub for managing distribution channels, enabling real-time data-sharing, collaboration, and decision-making among stakeholders, regardless of their geographic location. This seamless connectivity and access to critical information facilitate rapid response times and coordinated efforts during disruptions, minimising downtime and maintaining business continuity.

Moreover, cloud computing offers robust disaster recovery capabilities and redundancy, ensuring data and systems are backed up and can be quickly restored in the event of a disruption. The scalability of cloud resources allows companies to rapidly adjust their computing power, storage, and network capacity to meet fluctuating demands, ensuring resilience in the face of unexpected spikes or changes in distribution requirements.

Technology and Innovation for Resilient Distribution Channels (Continued)

Digital Twins: Digital twins, or virtual replicas of physical assets, processes, or systems, provide a powerful tool for enhancing the resilience of distribution channels. By creating digital representations of their distribution networks, companies can simulate various scenarios and, test strategies and identify potential vulnerabilities or bottlenecks without disrupting actual operations.

Digital twins leverage data from IoT sensors, historical data, and computational models to create accurate virtual representations of distribution channels. These digital replicas enable companies to visualise complex systems, analyse the impact of potential disruptions, and optimise processes through simulations and what-if analyses.

By simulating disruptions such as supply shortages, transportation delays, or changes in demand patterns, companies can evaluate the resilience of their distribution channels and identify areas for improvement. Digital twins also facilitate collaboration among stakeholders, allowing them to collectively explore alternative scenarios, test contingency plans, and make data-driven decisions to enhance the overall resilience of distribution channels.

Furthermore, digital twins can be integrated with predictive analytics and machine learning algorithms, enabling continuous optimisation and adaptation of distribution strategies based on real-time data and simulated outcomes.

Conclusion

In the face of an increasingly complex and volatile business environment, resilience within distribution channels has become a strategic imperative for organisations striving to maintain operational continuity, adapt to disruptions, and drive sustainable growth. This chapter has explored the multifaceted dimensions of resilience, highlighting the critical role of diversification, redundancy, agility, and collaboration in fortifying distribution channels.

By adopting a proactive and holistic approach to resilience planning, companies can anticipate risks, develop contingency plans, and build a robust foundation for effective crisis management. Leveraging cutting-edge technologies such as supply chain visibility, predictive analytics, cloud computing, and digital twins empowers organisations to enhance transparency, agility, and data-driven decision-making, enabling them to respond swiftly and effectively to disruptions.

Building resilient distribution channels is not a one-time endeavour but a continuous journey that requires a commitment to innovation, collaboration, and continuous improvement. By fostering a culture of resilience and embracing technological advancements, companies can not only mitigate risks but also seize opportunities, drive operational excellence, and gain a competitive edge in the ever-changing global marketplace.

Resilience within distribution channels serves as a catalyst for innovation, growth, and sustained success, empowering companies to thrive amidst uncertainties and emerge stronger from adversity. By implementing the strategies and practices outlined in this chapter, organisations can fortify their distribution channels, safeguard their operations, and position themselves for long-term success in today's dynamic business environment.

CHAPTER 11

LEVERAGING TECHNOLOGY IN CHANNEL MANAGEMENT

Introduction to Technological Advancements in Channel Management

In today's fast-paced business environment, the integration of cutting-edge technologies into channel management practices has become a game-changer for organisations seeking to gain a competitive edge and deliver exceptional customer experiences. This introductory section underscores the pivotal role of technology in reshaping traditional distribution processes and customer engagement strategies within the realm of channel management.

The rapid pace of technological advancements has disrupted traditional business models, prompting companies to embrace innovative solutions to streamline their channel management operations. By leveraging the power of technology, organisations can achieve unprecedented levels of efficiency, agility, and customer-centricity, thereby enhancing their ability to navigate the complexities of modern distribution channels effectively.

This chapter serves as a gateway to exploring the transformative impact of technology on channel management practices. It aims to provide a comprehensive overview of the specific technological advancements that have revolutionised the way companies manage their distribution channels, engage with customers, and optimise their overall channel management processes.

Through a detailed examination of cutting-edge technologies, such as artificial intelligence, machine learning, blockchain, the Internet of Things (IoT), and advanced analytics, this chapter will shed light on how these innovations are reshaping channel management strategies and operations. It will delve into the practical applications of these technologies, highlighting their potential to streamline supply chain management, enhance partner collaboration, improve inventory management, and deliver personalised customer experiences across multiple touchpoints.

Moreover, this chapter will explore the implications of technological advancements on channel partner relationships, emphasising the importance of fostering seamless integration and collaboration between various stakeholders within the distribution network. It will also address the challenges and opportunities presented by the integration of technology, providing insights into best practices for successful implementation and adoption.

By the end of this chapter, readers will gain a comprehensive understanding of the transformative potential of technology in channel management, equipping them with the knowledge and insights necessary to navigate the dynamic landscape of modern distribution channels and capitalise on the benefits of technological advancements.

The Transformative Role of Data Analytics

Harnessing the Power of Data Analytics in Channel Management

In the era of big data and digital transformation, data analytics has emerged as a powerful ally for companies seeking to optimise their channel management strategies and operations. By harnessing the wealth of data generated across various touchpoints, organisations can gain invaluable insights into customer behaviour, market trends, and operational performance, enabling them to make informed decisions and stay ahead of the competition.

The role of data-driven decision-making in channel management cannot be overstated. By leveraging advanced analytics tools and techniques, companies can analyse vast amounts of data from diverse sources, including sales records, customer interactions, supply chain operations, and market intelligence. This analytical prowess empowers organisations to identify patterns, uncover opportunities, and pinpoint areas for improvement, ultimately leading to more effective channel strategies and improved supply chain visibility.

Predictive analytics, in particular, has revolutionised channel management practices by enabling companies to anticipate future demand accurately. By analysing historical data and incorporating various factors such as seasonal trends, market conditions, and customer preferences, predictive models can forecast demand patterns with remarkable precision. This capability allows organisations to optimise inventory levels, reducing the risk of stockouts and overstocking, resulting in significant cost savings and improved customer satisfaction.

Furthermore, real-time data analytics plays a crucial role in monitoring channel performance and identifying trends as they unfold. By continuously analysing data streams from various sources, including point-of-sale systems, social media platforms, and customer feedback channels, companies can quickly detect changes in customer preferences, market dynamics, and potential risks. This real-time visibility enables organisations to respond swiftly to emerging challenges and capitalise on new opportunities, ensuring agility and adaptability in their channel management strategies.

Real-world examples and case studies provide compelling evidence of the transformative power of data analytics in channel management. For instance, a leading customer electronics retailer leveraged advanced analytics to optimise its supply chain operations, resulting in a 25% reduction in inventory levels and a significant improvement in customer satisfaction scores. Another example involves a global apparel brand that used predictive analytics to forecast demand accurately, enabling it to streamline its distribution channels and minimise stockouts during peak seasons.

By embracing data analytics, companies can unlock a wealth of insights and drive operational efficiencies, informed decision-making, and enhanced customer experiences within their channel management practices. As data continues to proliferate and analytical capabilities advance, the potential for data-driven channel management strategies will only continue to grow, positioning those who embrace this paradigm shift as leaders in their respective industries.

1. Walmart's Supply Chain Optimisation:

Walmart, the retail giant, has been at the forefront of leveraging data analytics to optimise its supply chain and channel management processes. By analysing vast amounts of data from various sources, including sales records, inventory levels, and customer preferences, Walmart has been able to forecast demand accurately and streamline its distribution channels. This approach has enabled the company to reduce stockouts, minimise excess inventory, and ensure that the right products are available at the right locations, leading to improved customer satisfaction and significant cost savings.

2. Amazon's Predictive Demand Forecasting:

Amazon, the e-commerce behemoth, is renowned for its sophisticated data analytics capabilities. The company utilises predictive analytics to forecast demand for its products across various channels, including its online platform and physical retail stores. By analysing historical data, customer behaviour patterns, and external factors such as seasonal trends and market conditions, Amazon can accurately predict demand and adjust its inventory levels accordingly. This approach has enabled the company to optimise its supply chain, reduce waste, and provide seamless customer experiences across multiple touchpoints.

3. Starbucks' Customer Insights and Personalisation:

Starbucks has leveraged data analytics to gain valuable insights into customer preferences and behaviour, enabling the company to deliver personalised experiences across its distribution channels. By analysing data from its loyalty programme, mobile app, and in-store transactions, Starbucks can identify individual customer preferences, tailor promotions, and offer personalised recommendations. This data-driven approach has not only enhanced customer satisfaction but also contributed to increased sales and customer loyalty.

4. Nike's Demand Sensing and Channel Optimisation:

Nike, the global sportswear brand, has embraced data analytics to optimise its channel management processes. The company employs demand sensing techniques, which involve analysing real-time data from various sources, including sales data, social media sentiment, and market trends. This approach allows Nike to quickly identify changes in customer demand and adjust its production and distribution strategies accordingly. By aligning its channel operations with real-time demand, Nike can minimise excess inventory, reduce stockouts, and ensure that the right products are available through the appropriate channels.

5. Unilever's Supply Chain Visibility and Risk Mitigation:

Unilever, a multinational customer goods company, has leveraged data analytics to enhance supply chain visibility and mitigate risks across its distribution channels. By analysing data from various sources, including supplier performance, logistics operations, and market conditions, Unilever can identify potential disruptions and bottlenecks in its supply chain. This proactive approach enables the company to implement contingency plans, adjust production schedules, and reallocate resources as needed, ensuring uninterrupted product availability and minimising the impact on customer satisfaction.

These examples demonstrate how leading companies across diverse industries have embraced data analytics to drive operational efficiencies, enhance customer experiences, and gain a competitive edge in their respective markets. By leveraging the power of data and advanced analytical techniques, organisations can optimise their channel management strategies, respond to changing market dynamics, and deliver superior value to their customers.

The Rise of E-commerce Platforms

The Rise of E-Commerce and Its Impact on Channel Management

The advent of e-commerce platforms has ushered in a transformative era for the retail industry, revolutionising the way businesses approach channel management and customer engagement. As online shopping experiences continue to evolve, companies are presented with unprecedented opportunities to reach global markets, personalise customer experiences, and drive sales growth through digital channels.

The proliferation of online shopping channels has disrupted traditional brick-and-mortar retail, compelling businesses to adapt and embrace omnichannel strategies. Customers now expect seamless and integrated shopping experiences across multiple touchpoints, blurring the lines between physical and digital channels. This shift has forced companies to rethink their channel management practices, prioritising the harmonisation of online and offline channels to deliver a cohesive and engaging customer journey.

One of the most significant impacts of e-commerce platforms is the ability to enable direct-to-customer (D2C) sales, bypassing traditional intermediaries and reducing distribution costs. By establishing a direct connection with customers through their online storefronts, companies can streamline their supply chains, gain greater control over pricing and promotions, and capture valuable customer data for targeted marketing and personalisation efforts.

The importance of omnichannel retailing in this digital age cannot be overstated. Customers expect a unified and consistent experience across all channels, whether browsing online, making purchases via mobile apps, or visiting physical stores. Companies that successfully integrate their online and offline channels can unlock a competitive advantage by providing customers with the convenience of seamless shopping experiences tailored to their preferences and needs.

E-commerce platforms have also opened up new avenues for companies to expand their market reach, transcending geographical boundaries and tapping into global customer bases. With the click of a button, businesses can showcase their products and services to a worldwide audience, leveraging the power of digital marketing and data-driven targeting strategies to attract and retain customers across multiple regions.

Case studies and real-world examples illustrate the transformative impact of e-commerce on channel management practices. For instance, a leading fashion retailer leveraged an omnichannel strategy, integrating its online store with its physical locations, allowing customers to browse, purchase, and pick up or return items seamlessly across channels. This approach resulted in a significant increase in customer loyalty and a notable boost in overall sales.

Another example involves a niche customer electronics brand that embraced D2C sales through its e-commerce platform, cutting out traditional distribution intermediaries. By engaging directly with customers and leveraging data-driven personalisation techniques, the company not only reduced operational costs but also fostered stronger brand loyalty and customer advocacy.

As e-commerce continues to evolve and customer expectations shift, companies that effectively leverage e-commerce platforms and embrace omnichannel strategies will be well-positioned to drive revenue growth, enhance customer experiences, and gain a competitive edge in the dynamic landscape of modern channel management.

Here are some case studies and real-world examples that demonstrate the transformative impact of e-commerce on channel management practices:

1. Nike's Direct-to-Customer Strategy:

Nike has significantly invested in its e-commerce platform and direct-to-customer (D2C) strategy, allowing the company to bypass traditional retail channels and connect directly with customers. Through its online store and mobile apps, Nike can personalise product recommendations, offer exclusive releases, and provide a seamless omnichannel experience. This approach has enabled Nike to strengthen its brand loyalty, gather valuable customer data, and drive sales growth while reducing reliance on third-party retailers.

2. Warby Parker's Vertically Integrated Model:

Warby Parker, a disruptive eyewear brand, has leveraged e-commerce to revolutionise the traditional eyewear industry. By adopting a vertically integrated model, Warby Parker manages the entire value chain, from product design and manufacturing to distribution through its e-commerce platform and select physical stores. This approach has allowed the company to offer high-quality products at affordable prices, bypass intermediaries, and deliver an exceptional customer experience through its seamless online and offline channels.

3. Sephora's Omnichannel Retail Experience:

Sephora, a leading cosmetics and beauty retailer, has successfully integrated its e-commerce platform with its physical stores, creating a seamless omnichannel experience for customers. Shoppers can browse and purchase products online, check in-store inventory, and even scan items in-store to access ratings, reviews, and tutorials. Sephora's omnichannel strategy has enhanced customer engagement, fostered brand loyalty, and driven sales growth across all channels.

4. Bonobos' Showroom Experience:

Bonobos, a men's apparel brand, has disrupted traditional retail by combining e-commerce with a unique showroom experience. Customers can visit Bonobos' physical showrooms, try on clothes, and place orders through online channels. This innovative approach reduces the need for extensive inventory at physical locations while providing a personalised shopping experience. By leveraging e-commerce and data analytics, Bonobos can optimise its supply chain and deliver a seamless customer journey across digital and physical touchpoints.

5. Amazon's Marketplace and Fulfilment Services:

Amazon's e-commerce platform has transformed channel management by enabling third-party sellers to reach a vast customer base and leverage Amazon's logistics and fulfilment services. Through its Marketplace and Fulfilment by Amazon (FBA) programmes, Amazon has created an ecosystem that allows businesses of all sizes to streamline their distribution channels, expand their market reach, and benefit from Amazon's robust e-commerce infrastructure.

These examples showcase how companies across various industries have embraced e-commerce platforms to reinvent their channel management strategies, optimise their supply chains, and deliver exceptional customer experiences. By leveraging the power of digital technologies, data analytics, and omnichannel approaches, these businesses have gained a competitive edge in the rapidly evolving retail landscape.

Harnessing the Power of Artificial Intelligence

Unleashing the Power of Artificial Intelligence in Channel Management

The rapid advancement of artificial intelligence (AI) technologies has ushered in a new era of innovation and disruption across various industries, and channel management is no exception. Companies are increasingly recognising the transformative potential of AI in optimising their channel management processes, anticipating customer needs, and driving operational efficiencies.

At the core of AI's impact on channel management lies its ability to analyse vast amounts of data and identify intricate patterns that would be challenging for human analysts to discern. AI-powered algorithms can process and interpret large datasets encompassing customer interactions, purchase histories, market trends, and supply chain operations, enabling companies to gain valuable insights into customer behaviour and preferences.

This predictive capability empowers businesses to anticipate customer needs proactively, tailor their marketing strategies, and deliver personalised experiences across multiple channels. By leveraging AI-driven predictive analytics, companies can forecast demand patterns, optimise inventory levels, and make data-driven decisions that enhance customer satisfaction while minimising operational costs.

Moreover, AI-driven chatbots and virtual assistants are revolutionising the way companies engage with customers across various channels. These intelligent systems can provide round-the-clock support, answering inquiries, resolving issues, and guiding customers through the purchasing process seamlessly. By automating routine tasks and offering personalised assistance, AI-powered chatbots and virtual assistants enhance customer service quality, reduce response times, and free up human resources to focus on more complex tasks.

The impact of AI extends beyond customer engagement, as AI-powered recommendation engines are transforming the way companies personalise product recommendations and drive cross-selling and upselling opportunities. By analysing customer data, purchase histories, and browsing patterns, these intelligent systems can suggest relevant products, accessories, and complementary items tailored to individual preferences. This level of personalisation not only enhances the customer experience but also contributes to increased sales and customer loyalty.

Real-world examples and case studies illustrate the transformative power of AI in channel management. For instance, a leading e-commerce platform leveraged AI-powered recommendation engines to personalise product suggestions, resulting in a significant increase in average order value and customer retention rates. Another example involves a multinational retailer that implemented AI-driven chatbots to streamline customer service operations, reducing response times and improving customer satisfaction scores.

As AI technologies continue to evolve, their applications in channel management will become increasingly sophisticated and far-reaching. Companies that embrace AI and integrate it into their channel management strategies will be well-positioned to stay ahead of the competition, delivering exceptional customer experiences, optimising operational efficiencies, and driving sustainable growth in the ever-changing business landscape.

Here are some real-world examples and case studies that demonstrate the transformative power of AI in channel management:

1. Stitch Fix's AI-Driven Personal Styling:

Stitch Fix, an online personal styling service, utilises AI to analyse customer preferences, body measurements, and style profiles to curate personalised clothing selections. Their AI algorithms learn from customer feedback and incorporate data from human stylists to continuously refine and improve their recommendations, leading to increased customer satisfaction and loyalty.

2. Nordstrom's AI-Powered Chatbot:

Nordstrom, a renowned fashion retailer, has implemented an AI-powered chatbot named "Nordstrom+Botmaker" to enhance customer service across multiple channels. The chatbot can assist customers with product recommendations, order tracking, and general inquiries, providing a seamless and personalised experience while reducing the workload on human customer service representatives.

3. Coca-Cola's AI-Driven Supply Chain Optimisation:

Coca-Cola has leveraged AI technologies to optimise its supply chain operations and channel management processes. The company uses AI algorithms to analyse sales data, weather patterns, and customer behaviour to forecast demand accurately and adjust production and distribution accordingly. This AI-driven approach has led to improved inventory management, reduced stockouts, and enhanced operational efficiencies.

4. L'Oréal's AI-Powered Product Recommendations:

L'Oréal, a global cosmetics company, has implemented AI-powered product recommendation engines across its various brands and channels. By analysing customer data, skin types, and preferences, L'Oréal's AI system can suggest personalised product recommendations, enhancing the customer experience and driving sales growth.

These examples showcase how companies across diverse industries are leveraging AI technologies to revolutionise their channel management practices, from personalised product recommendations and virtual shopping experiences to optimised supply chain operations and intelligent customer service. By embracing AI, these businesses are able to anticipate customer needs, streamline operations, and gain a competitive edge in their respective markets.

Enhancing Supply Chain Visibility with Blockchain

Blockchain Technology: Revolutionising Channel Management and Supply Chain Transparency

In the rapidly evolving landscape of channel management and supply chain operations, blockchain technology has emerged as a game-changing innovation, offering companies unprecedented levels of transparency, traceability, and security. This disruptive technology holds the potential to transform traditional processes, enabling businesses to track and authenticate products, streamline transactions, and mitigate risks across their distribution networks.

At its core, blockchain technology is a decentralised, distributed digital ledger that records transactions in a secure, transparent, and immutable manner. This revolutionary concept eliminates the need for a central authority, allowing participants to verify and validate transactions without the involvement of intermediaries. By leveraging cryptographic principles, blockchain ensures data integrity, tamper-resistance, and traceability, making it an ideal solution for supply chain management and channel management applications.

One of the most significant applications of blockchain in channel management is enabling end-to-end visibility and traceability across the supply chain. From raw material sourcing to final product delivery, blockchain technology allows companies to track the movement of goods, record key events, and access real-time data about the provenance and authenticity of products. This level of transparency not only enhances supply chain efficiency but also builds customer trust by providing verifiable information about the origins and journey of the products they purchase.

Furthermore, blockchain-based smart contracts offer a powerful solution for automating and securing transactions between channel partners. These self-executing contracts, embedded with predefined rules and conditions, can facilitate secure and transparent exchanges of goods, services, and payments without the need for intermediaries. By eliminating manual processes and reducing the risk of errors or disputes, smart contracts streamline channel management operations, fostering trust and collaboration among supply chain participants.

Case studies and examples illustrate the transformative impact of blockchain technology on channel management practices. For instance, a leading luxury brand leveraged blockchain to combat counterfeiting and enhance supply chain transparency, enabling customers to verify the authenticity of their purchases through a secure digital ledger. Another example involves a global food supply chain company that implemented blockchain to track the movement of agricultural products from farm to table, ensuring food safety, traceability, and regulatory compliance.

As the adoption of blockchain technology continues to gain momentum, companies that embrace this innovative solution will be well-positioned to enhance supply chain transparency, reduce operational costs, mitigate risks, and build stronger relationships with customers and channel partners alike. By leveraging the inherent benefits of blockchain, such as immutability, decentralisation, and security, businesses can gain a competitive edge in the ever-changing landscape of channel management and supply chain operations.

Here are some case studies and examples that showcase the transformative impact of blockchain technology on channel management practices:

1. IBM Food Trust:

IBM Food Trust is a blockchain-based platform designed to enhance transparency, traceability, and food safety across the global food supply chain. Major retailers like Walmart and food companies like Nestlé and Dole have adopted this platform to track the movement of food products from farm to store shelves. By leveraging blockchain, these companies can quickly identify the source of contaminated products, facilitate targeted recalls, and provide customers with verifiable information about the origins and journey of their food.

2. Everledger and the Diamond Industry:

Everledger, a blockchain-based platform, is revolutionising the diamond industry by providing an immutable digital ledger that tracks the provenance and authenticity of diamonds. By recording every step in a diamond's journey, from mining to cutting and polishing, Everledger enables companies and customers to verify the ethical sourcing and authenticity of diamonds, mitigating the risk of fraud and promoting transparency throughout the supply chain.

3. Maersk and IBM's TradeLens:

TradeLens is a blockchain-based platform developed by Maersk, a global logistics company, and IBM. It aims to streamline international shipping processes by providing a secure and transparent digital platform for sharing real-time data and documentation among supply chain participants, including shipping companies, ports, and customs authorities. By leveraging blockchain technology, TradeLens enhances visibility, reduces delays, and improves operational efficiency across the entire logistics and distribution network.

4. Walmart's Food Traceability Initiative:

Walmart has been a pioneer in adopting blockchain technology for food traceability. In partnership with IBM, Walmart has implemented a blockchain-based system to track the movement of food products, such as leafy greens and mangoes, from farm to store shelves. This initiative has significantly reduced the time required to trace the origin of contaminated products from weeks to seconds, enabling Walmart to respond swiftly to potential food safety issues and maintain customer trust.

5. De Beers' Tracr:

Tracr is a blockchain-based platform developed by De Beers, the world's largest diamond producer, to track the journey of diamonds from mine to retail. By leveraging blockchain technology, Tracr provides immutable records of a diamond's provenance, ensuring transparency and ethical sourcing throughout the supply chain. This initiative not only builds customer trust but also helps combat the trade of conflict diamonds and promotes responsible sourcing practices.

6. VeChain and Supply Chain Management:

VeChain is a blockchain-based platform designed specifically for supply chain management applications. Companies across various industries, including fashion, automotive, and logistics, have adopted VeChain to enhance product traceability, authenticate products, and streamline supply chain operations. By leveraging blockchain technology, VeChain enables businesses to build trust, reduce counterfeit risks, and optimise their distribution channels.

These examples demonstrate the diverse applications of blockchain technology in enhancing supply chain transparency, traceability, and security across various industries. By embracing blockchain, companies can gain a competitive edge, build customer trust, and optimise their channel management practices in today's global marketplace.

Conclusion

The journey through the transformative impact of technological advancements on channel management practices has unveiled a world of endless possibilities and opportunities for businesses to thrive in the digital age. As we conclude this comprehensive exploration, it is evident that technology has emerged as a game-changer, reshaping the very fabric of how companies approach distribution processes, customer engagement, and operational efficiencies.

Throughout these pages, we have delved into the powerful roles played by data analytics, e-commerce platforms, artificial intelligence, and blockchain technology in revolutionising channel management strategies. The ability to harness the power of data-driven insights, leverage omnichannel experiences, implement AI-powered automation, and ensure supply chain transparency through blockchain has proven to be invaluable for companies seeking to gain a competitive edge.

The integration of these cutting-edge technologies has not only optimised distribution channels and streamlined operations but has also enabled businesses to deliver personalised and exceptional customer experiences, fostering brand loyalty and driving sustainable growth. By embracing data analytics, companies can make informed decisions, anticipate customer behaviour, and optimise resource allocation. E-commerce platforms have opened up new avenues for reaching global markets and enabling direct-to-customer sales, bypassing traditional intermediaries. Artificial intelligence has revolutionised personalisation, customer service, and operational automation, empowering businesses to anticipate customer needs and deliver tailored experiences. Blockchain technology has ushered in a new era of transparency, traceability, and trust, mitigating risks and building stronger relationships with channel partners and customers alike.

In this rapidly evolving digital landscape, it is imperative for companies to recognise technology as a strategic enabler and invest in developing digital capabilities to meet the ever-changing customer expectations and market demands. Embracing a technology-driven mindset and fostering a culture of continuous innovation will be crucial for organisations to stay ahead of the curve and maintain relevance in an increasingly digital world.

CHAPTER 12

REGULATORY COMPLIANCE
AND LEGAL CONSIDERATIONS

Navigating Regulatory Requirements

In today's complex business landscape, channel partner programmes must navigate a myriad of regulatory requirements to ensure compliance and avoid legal pitfalls. Understanding and adhering to relevant laws, regulations, and industry standards is crucial for the success and longevity of these partnerships. Failure to comply with applicable regulations can result in severe consequences, such as hefty fines, legal disputes, reputational damage, and even the termination of the partner programme.

One of the primary regulatory frameworks that channel partner programmes must consider is antitrust laws. These laws are designed to promote fair competition and prevent anticompetitive practices, such as price fixing, market allocation, and bid rigging. Channel partners must be cautious not to engage in any activities that could be perceived as collusive or restrictive of competition. For example, setting minimum resale prices or imposing exclusive dealing arrangements may be deemed as violations of antitrust laws. It is essential for companies to provide clear guidelines and training to their channel partners on antitrust compliance and to monitor their activities regularly to identify and address any potential issues.

Data privacy regulations are another critical area of compliance for channel partner programmes. With the increasing emphasis on data protection and customer privacy rights, regulations such as the General Data Protection Regulation (GDPR) in the European Union and the California Customer Privacy Act (CCPA) in the United States have imposed stringent requirements on how personal data is collected, processed, and shared. Channel partners who handle customer data on behalf of the company must adhere to these regulations and implement appropriate security measures to safeguard sensitive information. Companies must ensure that their channel partners have robust data protection policies and procedures in place and that they obtain necessary consent and provide required disclosures to customers.

In addition to antitrust and data privacy regulations, channel partner programmes must also comply with industry-specific guidelines and standards. For example, in the healthcare industry, channel partners must adhere to the Health Insurance Portability and Accountability Act (HIPAA) regulations, which govern the handling of protected health information. In the financial services industry, channel partners must comply with the Payment Card Industry Data Security Standards (PCI DSS) to ensure the secure processing and storage of credit card data. Companies must identify the relevant industry-specific regulations and ensure that their channel partners are aware of and compliant with these requirements.

Staying updated on regulatory changes is another critical aspect of maintaining compliance in channel partner programmes. Regulations are constantly evolving, and new requirements may be introduced that impact the programme's operations. For example, the recent introduction of the California Privacy Rights Act (CPRA) has expanded the scope of customer privacy rights and imposed additional obligations on businesses. Companies must have mechanisms in place to monitor regulatory developments, assess their impact on the channel partner programme, and adapt the programme accordingly to ensure ongoing compliance.

To proactively identify and address potential compliance risks, companies should conduct regular audits and assessments of their channel partner programme. These audits may involve reviewing partner agreements, assessing partner compliance with contractual obligations, and evaluating the effectiveness of training and monitoring processes. By conducting periodic assessments, companies can identify areas of non-compliance, implement corrective actions, and minimise the risk of legal and regulatory violations. In conclusion, navigating regulatory requirements is a critical aspect of developing and managing successful channel partner programmes. Companies must understand and adhere to applicable laws, regulations, and industry standards, such as antitrust laws, data privacy regulations, and industry-specific guidelines. Staying updated on regulatory changes and conducting regular compliance audits are essential for maintaining compliance and mitigating potential risks. By prioritising regulatory compliance, companies can build trust with their channel partners, protect their reputations, and ensure the long-term viability of their partner programmes.

Ensuring Legal Compliance in Channel Operations

Channel partner programmes involve a complex web of legal considerations that must be carefully managed to minimise risks and liabilities. Neglecting these legal aspects can lead to costly disputes, damaged relationships, and even legal action. Therefore, it is crucial for companies to prioritise legal compliance in their channel operations and develop robust strategies to address key legal issues.

One of the foundational elements of ensuring legal compliance in channel partnerships is effective contract management. A comprehensive partner agreement serves as the backbone of the relationship, outlining the roles, responsibilities, performance expectations, and compliance obligations of both parties. It is essential to invest time and resources in drafting clear and legally enforceable contracts that cover all relevant aspects of the partnership. Key components of a partner agreement may include scope of work, pricing and payment terms, performance metrics, intellectual property rights, confidentiality clauses, indemnification provisions, and termination procedures. By clearly defining these elements in the contract, companies can establish a solid legal framework for the partnership and minimise the risk of misunderstandings or disputes.

Dispute resolution is another critical aspect of legal compliance in channel operations. Despite best efforts to maintain positive relationships, conflicts and disagreements can arise between partners. Having a well-defined dispute resolution process in place can help resolve issues efficiently and prevent escalation. The partner agreement should specify the steps and procedures for handling disputes, such as informal negotiation, mediation, or arbitration. It is important to establish clear communication channels and escalation paths to ensure that grievances are addressed promptly and effectively. By providing a structured approach to dispute resolution, companies can minimise the impact of conflicts on the partnership and maintain a healthy working relationship.

Termination procedures are another key legal consideration in channel partner programmes. While partnerships are typically entered into with the intention of long-term collaboration, circumstances may arise that necessitate the termination of the relationship. It is crucial to have clear provisions in the partner agreement that outline the grounds for termination, notice periods, and the process for winding down the partnership. This may include clauses related to the return of confidential information, the handling of ongoing customer engagements, and the allocation of any remaining inventory or assets. By establishing well-defined termination procedures, companies can protect their interests and ensure a smooth transition in the event of a partnership dissolution.

Conducting thorough due diligence on potential partners is another essential risk mitigation strategy in channel operations. Before entering into a partnership, companies should carefully evaluate the background, reputation, financial stability, and legal compliance records of prospective partners. This may involve reviewing public records, conducting reference checks, and assessing the partner's ability to meet contractual obligations. By performing comprehensive due diligence, companies can identify potential red flags and make informed decisions about partnering with entities that align with their legal and ethical standards.

Ongoing monitoring of partner compliance is equally important to ensure the continued legal health of the channel programme. Companies should establish regular review processes to assess partner adherence to contractual terms, performance expectations, and legal requirements. This may involve conducting periodic audits, reviewing sales and inventory reports, and monitoring customer feedback. By proactively monitoring partner compliance, companies can identify and address any issues early on before they escalate into major legal challenges.

In conclusion, ensuring legal compliance in channel operations is a multifaceted endeavour that requires careful planning, robust contract management, effective dispute resolution mechanisms, clear termination procedures, thorough due diligence, and ongoing compliance monitoring. By prioritising these legal considerations and developing comprehensive strategies to address them, companies can minimise risks, protect their interests, and foster long-term, successful partnerships in their channel programmes.

Intellectual Property Protection

Intellectual property (IP) is a vital asset for any company, and protecting it is of utmost importance in channel partner relationships. Channel partners often have access to sensitive information, including trade secrets, proprietary technologies, and confidential data, which can be vulnerable to infringement or misappropriation. Failure to adequately safeguard IP rights can lead to significant financial losses, competitive disadvantages, and damage to a company's reputation. Therefore, it is crucial for companies to prioritise IP protection in their channel partnerships and implement robust strategies to mitigate risks.

One of the key elements of IP protection in channel partnerships is the development of comprehensive IP clauses in partner agreements. These clauses should clearly define the ownership and usage rights of IP assets, as well as the obligations and restrictions imposed on partners. Non-disclosure agreements (NDAs) are a critical component of IP protection, as they legally bind partners to maintain the confidentiality of sensitive information and prevent unauthorised disclosure. NDAs should specify the scope of confidential information covered, the duration of confidentiality obligations, and the consequences of breach. Licensing terms and usage restrictions should also be clearly outlined in the partner agreement, defining the permitted uses of IP assets and any limitations or conditions associated with their use.

In addition to contractual measures, companies should also consider implementing technological safeguards to protect IP shared with channel partners. Access controls, such as user authentication and role-based permissions, can help ensure that only authorised individuals have access to sensitive information. Data encryption is another effective measure to secure confidential data both in transit and at rest. By encrypting IP assets, companies can protect them from unauthorised access, interception, or tampering. It is important to establish secure communication channels and data storage systems to minimise the risk of IP leaks or breaches.

Providing IP training to channel partners is another crucial aspect of protecting intellectual property. Partners should be educated on the importance of IP protection, the specific IP assets they will be handling, and the proper procedures for using and safeguarding those assets. Training should cover topics such as confidentiality obligations, acceptable use policies, and reporting mechanisms for suspected IP violations. By raising awareness and promoting a culture of IP protection among partners, companies can reduce the risk of unintentional or malicious misuse of intellectual property.

Establishing clear guidelines and policies for the handling of IP assets is also essential for effective protection. These guidelines should outline the specific responsibilities and expectations for partners in relation to IP management. This may include procedures for accessing, storing, and distributing confidential information, as well as protocols for reporting and addressing any suspected IP infringement or misappropriation. By providing partners with a clear framework for IP handling, companies can minimise the risk of inadvertent or unauthorised disclosures.

Regular monitoring and auditing of partner compliance with IP protection measures is another important strategy. Companies should periodically review partner adherence to contractual obligations, assess the effectiveness of technological safeguards, and investigate any potential IP violations. This may involve conducting random audits, reviewing access logs, and monitoring partner communications and activities. By proactively monitoring compliance, companies can identify and address any IP-related issues promptly, minimising the potential for damage or loss.

In the event of IP infringement or misappropriation by a channel partner, companies should have well-defined procedures in place for enforcement and remediation. This may include provisions for immediate termination of the partnership, legal action to seek injunctive relief or damages, and notification to relevant authorities. It is important to act swiftly and decisively to protect IP rights and mitigate any potential harm to the company's interests.

In conclusion, protecting intellectual property is a critical priority in channel partner relationships. Companies must develop robust IP protection strategies that encompass contractual measures, technological safeguards, partner training, clear guidelines, regular monitoring, and enforcement procedures. By implementing a comprehensive approach to IP protection, companies can safeguard their valuable assets, maintain competitive advantages, and foster trust and confidence in their channel partnerships.

Mitigating Risks and Liabilities

Channel partner programmes offer numerous benefits, but they also expose companies to various risks and liabilities that can have significant financial and reputational consequences. Product liability claims, warranty issues, and damage to brand reputation are just a few examples of the potential risks associated with channel partnerships. Therefore, it is crucial for companies to proactively identify, assess, and mitigate these risks to protect their interests and ensure the success of their channel programmes.

Conducting thorough risk assessments is a critical first step in mitigating risks and liabilities in channel partnerships. Companies should evaluate potential partners' capabilities, financial stability, and compliance track records to determine their ability to meet quality standards, fulfil contractual obligations, and maintain ethical practices. This assessment may involve reviewing partners' financial statements, insurance coverage, and legal history, as well as conducting background checks and references. By carefully assessing potential risks upfront, companies can make informed decisions about partnering with entities that align with their risk tolerance and business objectives.

Insurance coverage is another important tool for mitigating risks and liabilities in channel partnerships. Errors and omissions (E&O) insurance, also known as professional liability insurance, can protect companies against claims of negligence, mistakes, or omissions in the services provided by channel partners. Product liability insurance can safeguard against claims of injuries or damages caused by defective products distributed through the channel. Companies should carefully review their insurance policies and ensure that they have adequate coverage for the specific risks associated with their channel programme. It may also be beneficial to require channel partners to maintain their own insurance coverage as a condition of the partnership agreement.

Implementing robust quality control measures is essential for minimising product-related risks and liabilities in channel partnerships. Companies should establish clear quality standards and specifications for the products distributed through their channel partners. This may involve implementing product testing and certification programmes to ensure that products meet safety and performance requirements. Regular quality audits and inspections should be conducted to verify that partners are adhering to established quality standards and procedures. By maintaining strict quality control measures, companies can reduce the risk of product defects, safety issues, and customer complaints.

Establishing clear guidelines for handling customer complaints, product recalls, and crisis management situations is another critical aspect of risk mitigation in channel partnerships. Companies should develop detailed protocols for responding to customer inquiries, complaints, and product issues in a timely and effective manner. This may involve providing partners with scripts, escalation procedures, and reporting requirements to ensure consistent and appropriate handling of customer concerns. In the event of a product recall or safety issue, companies should have well-defined procedures in place for notifying partners, coordinating recall efforts, and communicating with affected customers. By proactively planning for potential crisis situations, companies can minimise the impact on their reputation and maintain customer trust.

Ongoing monitoring and evaluation of channel partners' performance and compliance is crucial for identifying and addressing potential risks and liabilities. Companies should establish regular review processes to assess partners' adherence to quality standards, contractual obligations, and ethical practices. This may involve conducting periodic audits, reviewing customer feedback and complaint data, and monitoring partners' financial and legal standing. By proactively monitoring partner performance, companies can identify and address any issues early on before they escalate into major risks or liabilities.

In the event of a breach of contract, negligence, or other legal issues involving a channel partner, companies should have well-defined procedures in place for enforcement and remediation. This may include provisions for termination of the partnership, legal action to seek damages or indemnification, and notification to relevant authorities. It is important to act swiftly and decisively to protect the company's interests and mitigate any potential harm to its reputation or financial well-being.

In conclusion, mitigating risks and liabilities in channel partner programmes requires a proactive and comprehensive approach. Companies must conduct thorough risk assessments, secure adequate insurance coverage, implement robust quality control measures, establish clear guidelines for handling customer issues and crises, monitor partner performance and compliance, and have well-defined enforcement and remediation procedures in place. By prioritising risk mitigation strategies, companies can protect their assets, reputation, and financial stability while fostering successful and sustainable channel partnerships.

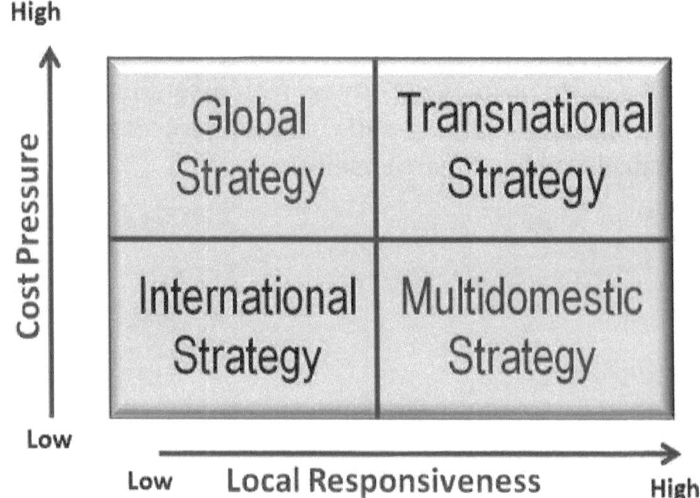

CHAPTER 13

CHANNEL EXPANSION AND INTERNATIONALISATION

Introduction

In today's increasingly interconnected and globalised business environment, channel expansion and internationalisation have become key drivers of growth and competitiveness for many companies. As markets become more saturated and customers demand more localised and specialised solutions, businesses are looking beyond their domestic borders to tap into new sources of revenue and diversify their customer base. However, expanding into new geographic markets is not without its challenges. Different countries and regions have unique cultural, linguistic, regulatory, and economic landscapes that can create significant barriers to entry and success. Companies must carefully assess the potential risks and rewards of internationalisation and develop strategic plans to navigate these complexities effectively.

One of the most critical decisions in channel expansion and internationalisation is choosing the right market entry strategy. Whether through direct sales, indirect channels, or a hybrid approach, companies must carefully consider the trade-offs between control, cost, and coverage in each target market.

They must also build the right partnerships and alliances to leverage local market knowledge, relationships, and infrastructure. Effective channel enablement and support are also essential to the success of international expansion efforts. Companies must provide their channel partners with the training, resources, and tools they need to effectively sell and support their products and services in local markets. They must also establish clear policies and processes to manage channel conflict and ensure consistent brand experiences across markets.

Finally, measuring and optimising channel performance is critical to ensuring the long-term success and sustainability of international channel networks. Companies must define clear metrics and KPIs that align with their global and local objectives and continuously monitor and adjust their channel strategies based on data-driven insights.

In this chapter, we will explore the key considerations and best practices for channel expansion and internationalisation. We will discuss how to identify and prioritise target markets, assess market entry strategies, overcome common challenges, and build and manage effective global channel networks. By the end of this chapter, readers will have a comprehensive understanding of how to develop and execute a successful international channel strategy that drives growth, profitability, and competitive advantage.

Exploring New Markets and Geographic Expansion

Expanding into new markets and geographies is a strategic move that can drive significant growth and diversification for companies. However, it requires a systematic and well-planned approach to identify the right opportunities, prioritise target markets, and develop an effective entry plan.

A. Identifying Growth Opportunities

The first step in exploring new markets is to identify potential growth opportunities. This involves:

1. Analysing market trends and customer needs: Companies must carefully study the market landscape, including demographic trends, customer preferences, and unmet needs. This can be done through market research, customer surveys, and analysis of industry reports and data.

2. Assessing competitive landscape and market saturation: It is essential to evaluate the competitive dynamics in each potential market, including the number and strength of existing players, their market share, and their competitive advantages. This helps determine whether there is room for new entrants and what unique value proposition is needed to succeed.

3. Evaluating economic, political, and regulatory factors: Companies must also consider the broader economic, political, and regulatory environment in each market. This includes factors such as economic stability, growth rates,

trade policies, investment incentives, and legal and regulatory frameworks that may impact business operations and profitability.

B. Prioritising Target Markets

Once potential growth opportunities have been identified, companies must prioritise which markets to pursue based on their strategic fit and potential return on investment. This involves:

1. Considering the market size, growth potential, and profitability: Companies should assess the overall size and growth trajectory of each market, as well as the potential profitability, based on factors such as pricing, cost structure, and customer lifetime value.

2. Evaluating fit with product/service offerings and value proposition: It is important to consider how well a company's existing products or services align with the needs and preferences of customers in each market. This may require adapting or localising offerings to meet specific market requirements.

3. Assessing internal capabilities and resources for expansion: Companies must also honestly evaluate their own internal capabilities and resources to determine whether they have the necessary skills, expertise, and financial and human capital to successfully enter and compete in each market.

C. Developing A Market Entry Plan.

Once target markets have been prioritised, companies must develop a comprehensive market entry plan that outlines the key objectives, strategies, and tactics for successful expansion. This includes:

1. Setting clear objectives and success metrics: Companies should define specific, measurable, achievable, relevant, and time-bound (SMART) objectives for each target market, such as revenue growth, market share, customer acquisition, or profitability targets. They should also establish clear success metrics to track progress and performance.

2. Allocating budget and resources: Based on the objectives and strategies, companies must allocate sufficient financial, human, and technological resources to support market entry and ongoing operations. This may require significant upfront investments in market research, product development, sales and marketing, and local infrastructure.

3. Defining timelines and milestones: Finally, companies should establish clear timelines and milestones for each phase of the market entry process, from initial planning and preparation to launch and post-launch optimisation. This helps ensure that all stakeholders are aligned and accountable for delivering results on schedule.

By following this structured approach to exploring new markets and geographic expansion, companies can make informed decisions about where and how to grow their business while minimising risk and maximising return on investment.

Assessing Market Entry Strategies

Once a company has identified and prioritised target markets for expansion, the next critical decision is choosing the most effective market entry strategy. There are several common approaches, each with its own advantages and trade-offs.

A. Direct Sales Model

One option is to establish a direct sales presence in the target market. This involves:

1. Building an in-house sales team: Companies can hire and train local sales representatives who deeply understand the market and can build direct relationships with customers. This provides a high degree of control over the sales process and customer experience.

2. Establishing local presence and infrastructure: To support a direct sales model, companies may need to invest in local offices, warehouses, and logistics capabilities. This can be a significant upfront investment but can also provide a strong foundation for long-term growth.

3. Maintaining control over brand and customer experience: With a direct sales model, companies have more ability to control messaging, positioning, and customer interactions. This can be especially important for complex or high-touch products and services.

B. Indirect Channel Model

Another common approach is to enter a new market through indirect channels, such as local partners or distributors. This involves:

1. Leveraging local partners and distributors: By partnering with established local players, companies can quickly gain access to their customer relationships, market knowledge, and distribution networks. This can be especially valuable in markets with high barriers to entry or complex regulatory environments.

2. Accessing established customer relationships and market knowledge: Local partners often have deep insights into customer needs, preferences, and buying behaviours. They can also provide valuable feedback on product fit and localisation requirements.

3. Enabling faster and more cost-effective scale-up: By leveraging existing partner infrastructure and resources, companies can often achieve faster time to market and lower upfront costs compared to building a direct presence from scratch.

C. Hybrid Or Multi-channel Approach

In many cases, the most effective market entry strategy may be a hybrid or multi-channel approach that combines elements of both direct and indirect models. This involves:

1. Combining direct and indirect channels based on market characteristics: Companies may choose to use direct sales for certain customer

segments or product lines while leveraging partners for others. The optimal mix will depend on factors such as customer preferences, product complexity, and market maturity.

2. Tailoring channel mix to customer segments and product lines: Different customer segments may require different levels of support and engagement. For example, large enterprise customers may require a direct sales approach, while small and medium-sized businesses may be better served through local partners.

3. Balancing control, cost, and coverage considerations: In a hybrid model, companies must carefully balance the trade-offs between control, cost, and market coverage. This may require establishing clear rules of engagement and incentive structures to ensure that all channels are aligned and motivated to drive growth.

Ultimately, the choice of market entry strategy will depend on a company's specific goals, resources, and risk tolerance. By carefully assessing the pros and cons of each approach and adapting to local market conditions, companies can position themselves for success in new geographic markets.

Overcoming Challenges in Internationalisation

Expanding into international markets can present a range of challenges that companies must navigate effectively to succeed. These challenges can be broadly categorised into cultural and language barriers, regulatory and compliance issues, and logistical and operational complexities.

A. Cultural And Language Barriers

One of the most significant challenges in internationalisation is bridging cultural and language gaps. This involves:

1. Adapting sales and marketing messages to local context: Companies must ensure that their messaging, branding, and value propositions resonate with local customers and are culturally appropriate. This may require significant localisation and adaptation of marketing materials, product packaging, and customer support resources.

2. Providing language support and training for channel partners: To effectively engage with local customers and partners, companies must provide language support and training. This may involve hiring local language speakers, providing translation and interpretation services, and developing multilingual sales and marketing collateral.

3. Building cultural awareness and sensitivity among team members: To avoid cultural missteps and build strong relationships with local partners and customers, companies must invest in cultural

awareness and sensitivity training for their team members. This includes understanding local customs, business practices, and communication styles.

B. Regulatory And Compliance Issues

Another major challenge in internationalisation is navigating complex and varying regulatory and compliance requirements across different markets. This involves:

1. Navigating local laws, regulations, and business practices: Each country has its own unique legal and regulatory landscape that companies must navigate. This may include licensing and registration requirements, product safety and labelling regulations, data privacy and protection laws, and local labour and employment standards.

2. Ensuring compliance with international trade and tax requirements: Companies must also ensure compliance with international trade and tax laws, including tariffs, duties, and export controls. This can be especially complex for companies dealing with physical goods and supply chain operations.

3. Protecting intellectual property and managing risk exposure: Intellectual property protection can also vary widely across different markets, and companies must take steps to safeguard their patents, trademarks, and trade secrets. This may require working with local legal experts and developing robust risk management strategies.

C. Logistical And Operational Complexities

Finally, internationalisation can create significant logistical and operational challenges that companies must overcome to maintain efficiency and customer satisfaction. This involves:

1. Establishing efficient supply chain and distribution networks: Companies must develop robust and efficient supply chain and distribution networks that can handle the complexity of cross-border operations. This may involve working with local logistics providers, establishing local warehousing and fulfilment capabilities, and optimising transportation and delivery routes.

2. Managing inventory, warranties, and returns across borders: International operations also require careful management of inventory levels, product warranties, and return policies across different markets. Companies must develop processes and systems to track and manage these issues effectively.

3. Providing timely and effective technical support and service: Finally, companies must ensure that they can provide timely and effective technical support and customer service across all markets. This may require investing in local service centres, partnering with local service providers, and developing robust remote support capabilities.

By proactively addressing these cultural, regulatory, and operational challenges, companies can position themselves for success in international markets.

This requires a strategic and adaptable approach that balances global consistency with local responsiveness and leverages the strengths of local partners and resources.

Building Global Channel Networks

Building a strong and effective global channel network is critical to the success of any international expansion strategy. This involves selecting the right partners, developing comprehensive enablement programmes, managing channel conflict and cannibalisation, and continuously measuring and optimising channel performance.

A. Selecting the right partners.

The first step in building a global channel network is selecting the right partners in each market. This involves:

1. Defining partner selection criteria and profile: Companies should establish clear criteria for what they are looking for in a partner, including industry expertise, market coverage, sales and technical capabilities, and alignment with their values and goals.

2. Conducting due diligence and background checks: Before entering into any partnership, companies should conduct thorough due diligence and background checks to verify the partner's credentials, financial stability, and reputation in the market.

3. Assessing partner capabilities, reputation, and cultural fit: Beyond the basic criteria, companies should also assess the partner's capabilities in areas such as marketing, customer support, and logistics. They should also consider the partner's reputation and cultural fit to ensure alignment and minimise potential conflicts.

B. Developing Partner Enablement Programmes.

Once partners have been selected, companies must invest in comprehensive enablement programmes to set them up for success. This involves:

1. Providing product and sales training: Partners must be thoroughly trained on the company's products, value proposition, and sales processes. This may involve a mix of in-person and online training, as well as ongoing coaching and support.

2. Offering marketing and demand generation support: Companies should also provide partners with marketing and demand generation support, including co-branded collateral, lead generation campaigns, and joint vents and promotions.

3. Implementing partner relationship management (PRM) systems: To streamline communication and collaboration with partners, companies should implement PRM systems that provide a centralised platform for sharing information, tracking performance, and managing incentives and rewards.

C. Managing Channel Conflict And Cannibalisation.

As companies expand their channel networks, they must also proactively manage potential channel conflict and cannibalisation. This involves:

1. Establishing clear rules of engagement and territory management: Companies should establish clear rules and guidelines for how partners should engage with customers and with

each other, including territory assignments and account ownership.

2. Implementing deal registration and lead distribution processes: To minimise channel conflict, companies should implement deal registration and lead distribution processes that ensure fair and transparent allocation of opportunities across partners.

3. Monitoring and enforcing policies to minimise channel friction: Companies should also closely monitor partner activities and enforce policies and procedures to minimise channel friction and maintain a positive partner ecosystem.

D. Measuring And Optimising Channel Performance.

Finally, to ensure the ongoing success and growth of their global channel networks, companies must continuously measure and optimise channel performance. This involves:

1. Defining global and local key performance indicators (KPIs): Companies should establish a set of global and local KPIs that align with their overall business objectives and provide a clear framework for measuring partner performance.

2. Implementing consistent reporting and analytics across markets: To track progress against these KPIs, companies should implement consistent reporting and analytics processes across all markets, providing visibility into partner performance at both the global and local levels.

3. Continuously assessing and adjusting channel strategies based on results: Based on the insights generated through this reporting and analytics, companies should continuously assess and adjust their channel strategies to optimise performance and drive growth. This may involve reallocating resources, modifying partner incentives, or exploring new partnerships or market opportunities.

By following these best practices for building and managing global channel networks, companies can establish a strong foundation for international success, leveraging the power of local partnerships to drive growth, profitability, and competitive advantage in new markets around the world.

Conclusion

In conclusion, channel expansion and internationalisation are critical strategies for companies looking to drive growth, diversify their customer base, and establish a global competitive advantage. However, success in new markets requires a systematic and well-planned approach that carefully considers the unique challenges and opportunities of each target geography.

To effectively explore new markets and prioritise expansion opportunities, companies must conduct thorough market research, assess the competitive landscape, and evaluate the fit with their existing products, services, and capabilities. They must also develop comprehensive market entry plans that set clear objectives, allocate appropriate resources, and define realistic timelines and milestones.

Choosing the right market entry strategy is also critical, whether through direct sales, indirect channels, or a hybrid approach. Each model has its own advantages and trade-offs in terms of control, cost, and market coverage, and the optimal mix will depend on the specific characteristics of each market and the company's goals and resources.

As companies expand internationally, they must also navigate a range of cultural, regulatory, and operational challenges. This requires adapting sales and marketing strategies to local contexts, ensuring compliance with complex legal and regulatory requirements, and establishing efficient and effective supply chain and support networks.

Building and managing a successful global channel network is also essential to long-term success. This involves selecting the right partners, investing in comprehensive enablement programmes, proactively managing channel conflict and cannibalisation, and continuously measuring and optimising channel performance.

Ultimately, the key to success in channel expansion and internationalisation is a strategic, adaptable, and customer-centric approach that balances global consistency with local responsiveness. By leveraging the power of local partnerships, market insights, and customer relationships, companies can unlock new sources of growth and establish a strong and sustainable competitive position in the global marketplace.

As the business landscape continues to evolve and new markets emerge, the ability to effectively expand and manage international channels will only become more critical. Companies that can master these strategies and build a truly global mindset will be well-positioned to thrive in an increasingly interconnected and competitive world.

CHAPTER 14

CHANNEL DISRUPTION AND INNOVATION

Introduction to Channel Disruption and Innovation

In today's dynamic business landscape, the concept of channel disruption and innovation has become increasingly pertinent as companies strive to remain competitive amidst rapid technological advancements and changing customer behaviours. This chapter serves as a comprehensive exploration of these phenomena, shedding light on the transformative forces reshaping traditional distribution channels.

Channel disruption and innovation encompass a wide array of developments, ranging from the proliferation of e-commerce platforms to the adoption of emerging technologies like blockchain and artificial intelligence. These disruptive forces challenge established distribution models, forcing companies to reassess their strategies and embrace innovative approaches to stay relevant in the market.

The impact of channel disruption and innovation is far-reaching, affecting industries across the board. From retail and manufacturing to healthcare and financial services, no sector is immune to the transformative effects of these phenomena. Companies that fail to adapt and innovate risk losing market share to more agile and forward-thinking competitors.

Throughout this chapter, we will delve into the underlying drivers of channel disruption, the impact of digital transformation on distribution channels, and the strategies companies can employ to harness innovation and thrive in an increasingly competitive landscape. We will examine real-world examples of companies that have successfully navigated channel disruption and those that have struggled to keep pace with the changing tides.

By the end of this chapter, readers will have a comprehensive understanding of channel disruption and innovation and be equipped with the knowledge and insights necessary to develop effective strategies for their own organisations. Whether you are a business leader, an entrepreneur, or a student of business, this chapter will provide you with a solid foundation for navigating the complex and ever-evolving world of channel disruption and innovation.

Understanding Channel Disruption

Channel disruption refers to the fundamental shifts and transformations occurring within distribution channels due to various factors, such as technological advancements, changing customer preferences, and evolving market dynamics. These disruptions fundamentally alter the way goods and services are bought, sold, and delivered, creating both challenges and opportunities for businesses.

Technological advancements, particularly in the realm of digitalisation, have been instrumental in driving channel disruption. The rise of e-commerce platforms, mobile applications, and other digital channels has revolutionised how customers interact with brands and make purchasing decisions. The convenience, accessibility, and personalisation offered by these digital channels have reshaped customer expectations and behaviours, forcing companies to adapt their distribution strategies accordingly.

Moreover, changing customer behaviours, such as the preference for online shopping and the demand for personalised experiences, have further accelerated the pace of channel disruption. Customers now expect seamless omnichannel experiences, where they can easily switch between online and offline channels throughout their purchasing journey. This shift has compelled companies to invest in digital capabilities and integrate their physical and digital channels to deliver a unified customer experience.

In addition to technological advancements and changing customer behaviours, evolving market dynamics also contribute to channel disruption. The emergence of new competitors, the blurring of industry boundaries, and the changing regulatory landscape can all disrupt traditional distribution channels and force companies to adapt their strategies.

Understanding the dynamics of channel disruption is crucial for companies seeking to navigate these transformative changes and capitalise on emerging opportunities in the market. By staying abreast of industry trends, monitoring competitor actions, and embracing innovation, companies can position themselves for success amidst channel disruption.

However, navigating channel disruption is not without its challenges. Companies must overcome organisational silos, legacy systems, and resistance to change to effectively adapt to the new realities of the market. They must also invest in the right technologies, talent, and partnerships to build the capabilities necessary to compete in a disruptive environment.

In the following sections, we will explore specific examples of channel disruption across various industries, delve into the strategies companies can employ to navigate disruption and discuss the role of innovation in driving growth and competitiveness in the face of channel disruption.

The Impact of Digital Transformation

Digital transformation lies at the heart of channel disruption, reshaping traditional distribution channels and driving new avenues for customer engagement and revenue generation. With the advent of digital technologies, companies have the opportunity to digitise their operations, optimise processes, and enhance the overall customer experience.

The impact of digital transformation on distribution channels is multifaceted. Digital channels, such as e-commerce platforms and mobile applications, offer companies unprecedented reach and accessibility to customers, enabling them to expand their market presence and drive sales growth. These channels provide customers with the convenience of shopping anytime, anywhere, and on any device, breaking down the barriers of time and location that traditionally limited customer access to products and services.

Moreover, digital transformation enables companies to gather valuable insights into customer behaviour, preferences, and purchasing patterns, allowing for more targeted and personalised marketing strategies. By leveraging data analytics and customer relationship management (CRM) systems, companies can gain a deeper understanding of their customers and tailor their offerings and communications accordingly. This level of personalisation enhances customer engagement, loyalty, and, ultimately, revenue growth.

The impact of digital transformation extends beyond customer-facing aspects to encompass supply chain management, logistics, and operational efficiency. By leveraging digital technologies, such as the Internet of

Things (IoT), artificial intelligence (AI), and blockchain, companies can streamline processes, improve inventory management, and enhance collaboration with channel partners. For example, IoT sensors can enable real-time tracking of inventory levels and supply chain movements, allowing for more efficient and responsive distribution strategies. AI-powered demand forecasting can help companies optimise their inventory management and reduce waste, while blockchain technology can enhance transparency and trust in supply chain transactions.

However, the adoption of digital technologies in distribution channels also presents challenges. Companies must invest in the necessary infrastructure, talent, and processes to effectively implement and manage digital transformation initiatives. They must also navigate the complexities of data privacy and security, ensuring the protection of customer information and compliance with relevant regulations.

Despite these challenges, the impact of digital transformation on distribution channels is undeniable. Companies that embrace digital technologies and adapt their strategies accordingly will be well-positioned to thrive in the face of channel disruption and capitalise on the opportunities presented by the digital age.

E-Commerce and Omnichannel Strategies

E-commerce has emerged as a major driver of channel disruption, offering customers unparalleled convenience, choice, and flexibility in their shopping experiences. The rise of online marketplaces, such as Amazon and Alibaba, has transformed the retail landscape, forcing traditional brick-and-mortar retailers to adapt and integrate e-commerce into their distribution strategies.

The benefits of e-commerce for companies are numerous. E-commerce platforms provide companies with access to a global customer base, allowing them to reach new markets and expand their business beyond traditional geographical boundaries. By leveraging the power of online marketplaces, companies can tap into existing customer bases and benefit from the trust and brand recognition associated with these platforms.

Moreover, e-commerce enables companies to gather rich data on customer behaviour, preferences, and purchasing patterns, allowing for more targeted and personalised marketing efforts. By analysing this data, companies can optimise their product offerings, pricing strategies, and promotional campaigns to better meet the needs and preferences of their customers.

However, the rise of e-commerce has also led to increased competition and price transparency, putting pressure on companies to differentiate themselves through factors beyond price alone. This has led to the emergence of omnichannel strategies, which seek to integrate online and offline channels to provide customers with seamless and cohesive experiences across multiple touchpoints.

Omnichannel strategies recognise that customers often engage with brands across various channels, including brick-and-mortar stores, websites, mobile apps, and social media platforms. By providing a consistent and personalised experience across these channels, companies can enhance customer engagement, loyalty, and, ultimately, sales.

For example, a customer may research a product online, visit a physical store to try it out, and then complete the purchase through a mobile app. An effective omnichannel strategy would ensure that the customer receives a seamless and consistent experience throughout this journey, with integrated inventory management, personalised recommendations, and unified customer support.

To successfully implement omnichannel strategies, companies must invest in the necessary technology infrastructure, such as integrated CRM systems, inventory management software, and data analytics tools. They must also foster a culture of collaboration and break down silos between online and offline teams to ensure a unified approach to customer engagement.

By embracing e-commerce and omnichannel strategies, companies can stay ahead of the curve in an increasingly digital marketplace and capitalise on the opportunities presented by channel disruption. However, the success of these strategies relies on a deep understanding of customer needs and preferences, as well as the ability to adapt and innovate in response to the ever-changing landscape of digital commerce.

Blockchain and Supply Chain Innovation

Blockchain technology has the potential to revolutionise supply chain management, offering transparency, security, and traceability across complex distribution networks. By leveraging blockchain, companies can create immutable records of transactions, track the movement of goods, and verify product authenticity throughout the supply chain.

One of the key advantages of blockchain is its ability to enhance trust and collaboration among supply chain partners. In traditional supply chain systems, each participant often maintains their own separate records, leading to discrepancies, disputes, and a lack of transparency. By providing a decentralised and transparent ledger of transactions, blockchain enables greater visibility into the flow of goods and the actions of participants, reducing the risk of fraud, counterfeiting, and other supply chain disruptions.

For example, in the food industry, blockchain can be used to track the origin and journey of products from farm to table, ensuring food safety and quality. By recording each step of the supply chain on the blockchain, companies can quickly identify and trace the source of any contamination or quality issues, minimising the impact of food recalls and protecting customer health.

Moreover, blockchain facilitates the automation of processes such as smart contracts, which can streamline transactions, enforce agreements, and reduce administrative overhead. Smart contracts are self-executing contracts with the terms of the agreement directly written into code. When predefined conditions are met, the contract automatically executes, triggering actions such as payments, product releases, or data transfers. This automation can greatly reduce the time and cost associated with traditional paper-based contracts and manual processes.

Another area where blockchain can drive supply chain innovation is in the realm of provenance and authenticity. By creating an immutable record of a product's journey through the supply chain, blockchain can help combat counterfeiting and ensure the authenticity of goods. This is particularly relevant for luxury goods, pharmaceuticals, and other high-value products where counterfeiting is a significant problem.

However, the adoption of blockchain in supply chain management is not without its challenges. Implementing blockchain solutions requires significant investment in technology infrastructure, as well as the collaboration and buy-in of all participants in the supply chain. There are also concerns about the scalability and energy consumption of certain blockchain platforms, which may limit their applicability in some contexts.

Despite these challenges, the potential benefits of blockchain for supply chain innovation are significant. By enabling greater transparency, trust, and efficiency, blockchain has the potential to transform the way companies manage their supply chains and interact with their partners. As the technology continues to mature and more companies explore its applications, we can expect to see further innovation and disruption in this space.

Artificial Intelligence and Predictive Analytics

Artificial intelligence (AI) and predictive analytics are transforming how companies analyse data, make decisions, and interact with customers. By leveraging AI algorithms and machine learning techniques, companies can extract valuable insights from vast amounts of data, enabling more informed and data-driven decision-making.

One of the key applications of AI in distribution channels is predictive analytics. Predictive analytics allows companies to anticipate customer needs, forecast demand, and optimise inventory management, leading to reduced costs and improved operational efficiency. By analysing historical data and identifying patterns, predictive analytics enables companies to make accurate predictions about future trends and behaviours, allowing for more proactive and targeted marketing strategies.

For example, predictive analytics can be used to forecast sales trends, identify high-value customers, and optimise pricing strategies. By analysing customer purchase history, browsing behaviour, and demographic data, companies can develop targeted marketing campaigns and personalised product recommendations that are more likely to resonate with individual customers.

AI-powered demand forecasting is another area where predictive analytics can drive significant value. By analysing past sales data, market trends, and external factors such as weather patterns and economic indicators, AI algorithms can generate accurate demand forecasts, enabling companies to optimise their inventory levels and avoid stockouts or overstocking.

In addition to predictive analytics, AI is also transforming the way companies interact with customers through chatbots and virtual assistants. By leveraging natural language processing and machine learning capabilities, chatbots can understand and respond to customer queries in real-time, providing instant support and guidance. This not only improves the customer experience but also frees up human agents to focus on more complex and high-value tasks.

AI-powered chatbots can also be used to personalise the customer experience and provide targeted product recommendations based on individual preferences and past interactions. By analysing customer data and engagement patterns, chatbots can deliver customised content and offers that are more likely to convert, driving sales growth and customer loyalty.

However, the adoption of AI and predictive analytics also presents challenges for companies. Developing and implementing AI solutions requires significant investment in data infrastructure, talent, and processes. Companies must also navigate ethical and privacy concerns around the use of customer data and ensure that their AI systems are transparent, fair, and unbiased.

Despite these challenges, the potential benefits of AI and predictive analytics for driving innovation and growth in distribution channels are immense. By leveraging these technologies, companies can gain deeper insights into customer behaviour, optimise operations, and deliver more personalised and engaging experiences across all touchpoints. As AI continues to advance and become more accessible, we can expect to see further disruption and transformation in the way companies approach distribution and customer engagement.

The Role of Startups and Disruptors

Startups and disruptors play a significant role in driving channel disruption and innovation, challenging established players and reshaping industry dynamics. By leveraging technology and innovative business models, startups are able to quickly iterate, experiment, and disrupt traditional distribution channels.

One of the key ways startups are disrupting distribution channels is through the rise of direct-to-customer (DTC) brands. DTC brands are bypassing traditional retail channels and selling directly to customers through digital platforms, allowing them to offer unique products, personalised experiences, and competitive pricing. By controlling the entire customer journey from manufacturing to delivery, DTC brands can gather valuable data on customer preferences and behaviours, enabling them to rapidly adapt their offerings and marketing strategies.

Subscription-based services are another example of disruptive business models pioneered by startups. By offering customers convenient, personalised, and often lower-cost alternatives to traditional purchasing models, subscription services are reshaping the way products are consumed and delivered. From meal kits and beauty products to software and entertainment, subscription services are disrupting a wide range of industries and forcing established players to rethink their distribution strategies.

Startups are also driving innovation in areas such as supply chain management, logistics, and last-mile delivery. By embracing new technologies such as drones, autonomous vehicles, and blockchain, startups are able to address inefficiencies and pain points within traditional distribution channels. For example, startups like Zipline are using drones to deliver medical supplies to remote areas, while companies like Convoy are using AI and machine learning to optimise freight transportation and reduce waste in the supply chain.

The impact of startups and disruptors on established players can be significant. Startups are often able to move faster, experiment more readily, and take risks that larger, more established companies cannot. This agility allows them to quickly identify and capitalise on new opportunities, forcing established players to adapt or risk being left behind.

However, established companies also have advantages that startups lack, such as scale, brand recognition, and resources. To stay competitive in the face of disruption, established players must find ways to leverage these advantages while also embracing innovation and agility. This may involve partnering with or acquiring startups, investing in research and development, and fostering a culture of experimentation and risk-taking.

Overall, the role of startups and disruptors in driving channel disruption and innovation cannot be overstated. As technology continues to evolve and customer expectations shift, startups will continue to push the boundaries of what is possible, reshaping industries and forcing established players to adapt and innovate in response.

Overcoming Challenges and Embracing Innovation

While channel disruption presents significant opportunities for growth and innovation, it also poses challenges for companies navigating rapid change and uncertainty. To thrive in this new landscape, companies must overcome organisational inertia, legacy systems, and cultural barriers to embrace innovation and adapt to new market realities.

One of the key challenges companies face is the need to foster a culture of innovation and experimentation. Many companies are constrained by rigid processes, siloed departments, and risk-averse cultures that stifle creativity and hinder innovation. To overcome these challenges, companies must create an environment that encourages experimentation, rewards risk-taking and embraces failure as a learning opportunity.

This may involve implementing new organisational structures, such as cross-functional teams or innovation labs, that bring together diverse perspectives and skill sets to solve complex problems. It may also require investing in employee training and development programmes that foster creativity, collaboration, and adaptability.

Another challenge is the need to develop the capabilities and infrastructure required to support innovation. This may involve investing in new technologies, such as cloud computing, AI, and blockchain, that enable faster, more efficient, and more secure distribution channels. It may also require hiring and training talent with the skills and expertise needed to develop and implement these technologies effectively.

In addition to technological challenges, companies must also address regulatory and compliance issues, privacy concerns, and cybersecurity risks associated with adopting new technologies and approaches. This may involve working closely with legal and compliance teams to ensure that new initiatives meet regulatory requirements and protect customer data.

To successfully navigate these challenges and embrace innovation, companies must take a holistic approach that encompasses people, processes, and technology. This may involve:

1. Developing a clear innovation strategy that aligns with business goals and priorities

2. Fostering a culture of experimentation and risk-taking that encourages creativity and collaboration

3. Investing in the right technologies and capabilities to support innovation and drive efficiency

4. Building partnerships and ecosystems with startups, technology providers, and other industry players to access new ideas and expertise

5. Continuously monitoring and adapting to changes in the market and customer needs

By taking a proactive and strategic approach to innovation, companies can not only overcome the challenges posed by channel disruption but also unlock new opportunities for growth and competitive advantage. As the pace of change continues to accelerate, the ability to embrace innovation and adapt to new market realities will be critical to long-term success in an increasingly dynamic and unpredictable business environment.

Conclusion

In conclusion, channel disruption and innovation are reshaping traditional distribution channels and creating new opportunities for businesses to engage with customers, streamline operations, and drive growth. The rise of e-commerce, the adoption of emerging technologies such as AI and blockchain, and the emergence of new business models like DTC and subscription services are all contributing to a rapidly evolving landscape that requires companies to be agile, adaptable, and innovative.

Throughout this chapter, we have explored the various dimensions of channel disruption and innovation, from the impact of digital transformation on customer expectations and experiences to the role of startups and disruptors in challenging established players and driving industry change. We have also examined the key technologies and strategies that companies can leverage to navigate disruption and unlock new opportunities for growth, such as omnichannel integration, predictive analytics, and supply chain optimisation.

However, succeeding in this new landscape is not just about adopting the latest technologies or business models. It also requires a fundamental shift in mindset and culture, one that embraces experimentation, risk-taking, and continuous learning. Companies that are able to foster a culture of innovation, empower their employees to think creatively and collaboratively, and build partnerships and ecosystems that bring together diverse perspectives and expertise will be best positioned to thrive in the face of disruption.

Looking ahead, the pace of change is only likely to accelerate as new technologies and business models continue to emerge and evolve. To stay ahead of the curve, companies must remain vigilant and proactive, continually monitoring industry trends, experimenting with new approaches, and adapting to changing customer needs and expectations.

By embracing digital transformation, adopting innovative technologies, and fostering a culture of innovation, companies can not only navigate the challenges of channel disruption but also unlock new opportunities for growth and competitive advantage. With a strategic focus on agility, adaptability, and customer-centricity, businesses can position themselves for success in an increasingly dynamic and unpredictable marketplace.

Ultimately, the future of distribution channels will be shaped by those companies that are able to effectively harness the power of innovation to create value for their customers, their employees, and their shareholders. By staying focused on these key priorities and continually pushing the boundaries of what is possible, businesses can thrive in the age of channel disruption and innovation, driving sustainable growth and success for years to come.

FINAL COMMENTS AND THOUGHTS

Reflections on the Journey of Channel Management

As we conclude this exploration of the intricacies and challenges of channel management, it's worth reflecting on the transformative journey businesses undertake when they embark on building and optimising their channel ecosystems. From the initial strategic decisions to the ongoing efforts in maintaining and growing these relationships, channel management is a complex and multifaceted endeavour that requires dedication, adaptability, and a deep understanding of the market dynamics at play.

Throughout this book, we have delved into the various aspects of channel management, examining best practices, common pitfalls, and the key drivers of success. We have seen how effective channel management, a powerful catalyst for business growth, can be, enabling companies to expand their reach, tap into new markets, and leverage the strengths of their partners to create mutual value.

However, we have also confronted the inherent challenges and risks associated with managing a complex network of intermediaries. From conflicts and misalignments to issues of control and transparency, the channel conundrum is a constant balancing act that requires careful navigation and a proactive approach to problem-solving.

Key Takeaways and Implications for Businesses

As businesses assess their channel management strategies and look to the future, there are several key takeaways and implications to consider:

1. **Embrace a customer-centric mindset:** Ultimately, the success of any channel strategy hinges on its ability to meet the evolving needs and preferences of the end customer. By placing the customer at the centre of decision-making and aligning channel efforts around delivering superior value, businesses can build stronger, more resilient ecosystems.

2. **Foster collaboration and trust:** Building strong, trust-based relationships with channel partners is essential for long-term success. By investing in open communication, joint problem-solving, and mutually beneficial incentive structures, companies can create a culture of collaboration that drives innovation and growth.

3. **Adapt and evolve:** The channel landscape is constantly shifting, driven by changing market dynamics, technological advancements, and evolving customer expectations. Businesses must remain agile and responsive, continuously adapting their strategies and tactics to stay ahead of the curve.

4. **Measure and optimise performance:** Effective channel management requires a data-driven approach to decision-making. By establishing clear metrics, tracking performance, and leveraging analytics to identify opportunities

for improvement, businesses can continuously refine their channel strategies and drive better outcomes.

Closing Remarks and Inspirational Insights

As we close this exploration of the channel conundrum, it's important to remember that success in channel management is not just about navigating challenges but also about seizing opportunities. By embracing the potential of collaborative partnerships, businesses can tap into new sources of innovation, expand their capabilities, and create value that extends far beyond what they could achieve on their own.

The journey of channel management is one of continuous learning, adaptation, and growth. It requires a willingness to take risks, to challenge assumptions, and to push beyond the boundaries of what is comfortable or familiar. But for those who are willing to embark on this journey, the rewards can be truly transformative.

As you reflect on the insights and strategies presented in this book, I encourage you to approach channel management with a spirit of curiosity, openness, and determination. Embrace the challenges as opportunities for growth, and never lose sight of the ultimate goal – to create value for your customers, your partners, and your business.

The channel ecosystem is a rich and dynamic landscape full of untapped potential and possibility. By navigating this landscape with skill, vision, and a commitment to collaboration, you can unlock new levels of success and achieve your most ambitious goals. So here's to the journey ahead – may it be filled with discovery, growth, and the realisation of your boldest aspirations.

In this era of continuous transformation, collaboration and partnership emerge as key drivers of success. By forging strategic alliances with channel partners, startups, and technology providers, companies can leverage collective expertise, resources, and insights to drive mutual value creation and foster a culture of innovation. These collaborative ecosystems enable businesses to stay at the forefront of industry trends, experiment with new approaches, and adapt to changing customer needs and preferences.

May this book serve not only as a repository of knowledge but also as a source of inspiration for businesses embarking on their journey toward channel excellence and market leadership. Together, let us confront the challenges and seize the opportunities of the digital frontier, paving the way for a brighter, more prosperous future for all.

In the end, the success of any business in the digital age will be determined by its ability to adapt, evolve, and innovate in the face of change. By embracing the insights and strategies presented in this book, companies can position themselves for long-term success, building resilient and agile distribution channels that can withstand the tests of time and disruption.

The future of channel management and innovation is ours to create, and with the right mindset, strategies, and collaborative spirit, there is no limit to what we can achieve.

GLOSSARY OF KEY TERMS AND DEFINITIONS

Channel Management: Channel management is not just about distributing products or services but involves the strategic planning, organisation, and control of distribution channels. It encompasses activities such as channel selection, partner management, logistics coordination, and performance evaluation.

1. **Channel**: A channel refers to the route or pathway through which products or services move from producers to customers. This includes the various intermediaries involved in the distribution process, such as wholesalers, retailers, distributors, agents, and online platforms.

2. **Channel Intermediaries**: These are entities positioned between manufacturers and end customers, facilitating the movement of goods or services. Intermediaries add value by providing services such as warehousing, transportation, marketing, and customer support.

3. **Direct Channel**: A direct channel involves the sale of products directly from manufacturers to customers without the involvement of intermediaries. This approach allows manufacturers to maintain control over pricing, branding, and customer relationships.

4. **Indirect Channel**: In contrast to direct channels, indirect channels utilise intermediaries like wholesalers, retailers, or distributors to distribute products to customers. Indirect channels are common in industries where manufacturers lack direct access to end customers.

5. **Hybrid Channel**: A hybrid channel combines elements of both direct and indirect distribution channels. It leverages multiple channels, including online and offline platforms, to reach diverse customer segments and optimise market coverage.

6. **Channel Strategy**: A channel strategy outlines a company's approach to managing distribution channels to achieve its business objectives. It encompasses decisions related to channel design, partner selection, pricing, promotion, and customer service.

7. **Channel Partner**: A channel partner collaborates with a manufacturer to distribute its products or services through the partner's existing distribution network. Partnerships can include retailers, distributors, resellers, agents, or franchisees.

8. **Channel Conflict**: Conflict may arise between channel members due to disagreements over issues such as pricing, territory rights, product placement, or promotional support. Effective conflict resolution strategies are crucial for maintaining channel harmony and performance.

9. **Channel Power**: Channel power refers to the ability of one channel member to influence the behaviour or decisions of other members. Power dynamics can affect negotiations, collaborations, and the overall effectiveness of distribution channels.

10. **Channel Performance**: Channel performance measures the effectiveness and efficiency of distribution channels in achieving strategic objectives such as market reach, sales growth, and customer satisfaction. Key performance indicators (KPIs) may include sales volume, market share, channel profitability, and customer retention.

11. **Channel Optimisation**: Channel optimisation involves continuously improving the performance and efficiency of distribution channels through strategic planning, resource allocation, and performance measurement. This may include streamlining processes, enhancing partner relationships, and leveraging technology.

12. **Channel Innovation**: Channel innovation entails adopting new technologies, processes, or strategies to enhance the effectiveness and competitiveness of distribution channels. This could involve implementing e-commerce platforms, optimising logistics, or introducing innovative partnership models.

13. **Channel Disruption**: Channel disruption refers to significant changes or transformations in distribution channels caused by factors such as technological advancements, shifting customer

behaviours, or competitive pressures. Companies must adapt to disruptions to remain competitive and relevant.

14. **Omnichannel Strategy**: An omnichannel strategy integrates multiple sales and distribution channels, such as online, offline, and mobile, to provide a seamless and consistent customer experience across all touchpoints. It requires effective coordination and integration of channels to meet customer expectations.

15. **Supply Chain Management**: Supply chain management involves the strategic management of the entire flow of goods or services, from sourcing raw materials to delivering the final product to customers. It encompasses activities such as procurement, production, inventory management, logistics, and distribution.

16. **Distribution Network**: A distribution network comprises the interconnected system of facilities, partners, and processes involved in the movement of products or services from manufacturers to end customers. It includes warehouses, distribution centres, transportation networks, and retail outlets.

17. **Channel Expansion**: Channel expansion involves expanding the reach and coverage of distribution channels by entering new markets, segments, or geographic regions. It may require partnerships, investments in infrastructure, and adaptation to local market conditions.

18. **Channel Partner Relationship Management (PRM)**: Channel PRM focuses on managing and nurturing relationships with channel partners to maximise mutual value and success. It involves activities such as partner recruitment, onboarding, training, communication, collaboration, and performance evaluation.

19. **Channel Analytics**: Channel analytics involves using data analysis and insights to measure, monitor, and optimise the performance of distribution channels. It includes tracking key metrics such as sales, inventory turnover, customer satisfaction, market share, and channel profitability to inform decision-making and drive continuous improvement.

REFERENCES

Anderson, E., & Narus, J. A. (1990). A model of distributor firm and manufacturer firm working partnerships. Journal of Marketing, 54(1), 42-58.

Bahadir, S. C., Bharadwaj, S. G., & Srivastava, R. K. (2015). Marketing mix and brand sales in global markets: Examining the contingent role of country-market characteristics. Journal of International Business Studies, 46(5), 596-619.

Gilliland, D. I. (2003). Toward a business-to-business channel incentives classification scheme. Industrial Marketing Management, 32(1), 55-67.

Griffith, D. A., & Dimitrova, B. V. (2014). Business and cultural aspects of psychic distance and complementarity of capabilities in export relationships. Journal of International Marketing, 22(3), 50-67.

Heide, J. B. (1994). Interorganizational governance in marketing channels. Journal of Marketing, 58(1), 71-85.

Kozlenkova, I. V., Samaha, S. A., & Palmatier, R. W. (2015). Resource-based theory in marketing. Journal of the Academy of Marketing Science, 43(1), 1-21.

Kumar, V., Chattaraman, V., Neghina, C., Skiera, B., Aksoy, L., Buoye, A., & Henseler, J. (2013). Data-driven services marketing in a connected world. Journal of Service Management, 24(3), 330-352.

Neslin, S. A., Grewal, D., Leghorn, R., Shankar, V., Teerling, M. L., Thomas, J. S., & Verhoef, P. C. (2006). Challenges and opportunities in multichannel customer management. Journal of Service Research, 9(2), 95-112.

Palmatier, R. W., Stern, L. W., & El-Ansary, A. I. (2016). Marketing channel strategy (8th ed.). Pearson.

Payne, A., & Frow, P. (2005). A strategic framework for customer relationship management. Journal of Marketing, 69(4), 167-176.

Samiee, S., Chabowski, B. R., & Hult, G. T. M. (2015). International relationship marketing: Intellectual foundations and avenues for further research. Journal of International Marketing, 23(4), 1-21.Verhoef, P. C., Kannan, P. K., & Inman, J. J. (2015). From multi-channel retailing to omni-channel retailing: Introduction to the special issue on multi-channel retailing. Journal of Retailing, 91(2), 174-181.

Wedel, M., & Kannan, P. K. (2016). Marketing analytics for data-rich environments. Journal of Marketing, 80(6), 97-121.

Beauchamp, M. B., & Barnes, D. C. (2015). Delighting baby boomers and millennials: Factors that matter most. Journal of Marketing Theory and Practice, 23(3), 338-350.

Brynjolfsson, E., Hu, Y. J., & Rahman, M. S. (2013). Competing in the age of omnichannel retailing. MIT Sloan Management Review, 54(4), 23-29.

Day, G. S., & Moorman, C. (2010). Strategy from the outside in: Profiting from customer value. McGraw-Hill.

Gielens, K., & Steenkamp, J. B. E. (2019). Branding in the era of digital (dis)intermediation. International Journal of Research in Marketing, 36(3), 367-384.

Haddud, A., DeSouza, A., Khare, A., & Lee, H. (2017). Examining potential benefits and challenges associated with the Internet of Things integration in supply chains. Journal of Manufacturing Technology Management, 28(8), 1055-1085.

Herhausen, D., Binder, J., Schoegel, M., & Herrmann, A. (2015). Integrating bricks with clicks: Retailer-level and channel-level outcomes of online-offline channel integration. Journal of Retailing, 91(2), 309-325.

Neslin, S. A., Grewal, D., Leghorn, R., Shankar, V., Teerling, M. L., Thomas, J. S., & Verhoef, P. C. (2006). Challenges and opportunities in multichannel customer management. Journal of Service Research, 9(2), 95-112.

Palmatier, R. W., Stern, L. W., & El-Ansary, A. I. (2016). Marketing channel strategy (8th ed.). Pearson.

Samiee, S., & Chabowski, B. R. (2012). Knowledge structure in international marketing: A multi-method bibliometric analysis. Journal of the Academy of Marketing Science, 40(2), 364-386.

Verhoef, P. C., Kannan, P. K., & Inman, J. J. (2015). From multi-channel retailing to omni-channel retailing: Introduction to the special issue on multi-channel retailing. Journal of Retailing, 91(2), 174-181.

Wedel, M., & Kannan, P. K. (2016). Marketing analytics for data-rich environments. Journal of Marketing, 80(6), 97-121.

References

Wiese, A., Kellner, J., Lietke, B., Toporowski, W., & Zielke, S. (2012). Sustainability in retailing - a summative content analysis. International Journal of Retail & Distribution Management, 40(4), 318-335.

Anderson, E., & Weitz, B. (1992). The use of pledges to build and sustain commitment in distribution channels. Journal of Marketing Research, 29(1), 18-34.

Brouthers, K. D., Brouthers, L. E., & Werner, S. (2008). Resource-based advantages in an international context. Journal of Management, 34(2), 189-217.

Cavusgil, S. T., Yeoh, P.-L., & Mitri, M. (2004). Selecting foreign distributors: An expert systems approach. Industrial Marketing Management, 24(4), 297-304.

Frazier, G. L., & Summers, J. O. (1984). Interfirm influence strategies and their application within distribution channels. Journal of Marketing, 48(3), 43-55.

Geigenmüller, A., & Bettis-Outland, H. (2012). Brand equity in B2B services and consequences for the trade show industry. Journal of Business & Industrial Marketing, 27(6), 428-435.

Gençtürk, E. F., & Aulakh, P. S. (2007). Norms- and control-based governance of international manufacturer-distributor relational exchanges. Journal of International Marketing, 15(1), 92-126.

Gilliland, D. I. (2003). Toward a business-to-business channel incentives classification scheme. Industrial Marketing Management, 32(1), 55-67.

Homburg, C., Workman, J. P., & Jensen, O. (2002). A configurational perspective on key account management. Journal of Marketing, 66(2), 38-60.

Jap, S. D., & Ganesan, S. (2000). Control mechanisms and the relationship life cycle: Implications for safeguarding specific investments and developing commitment. Journal of Marketing Research, 37(2), 227-245.

Kotler, P., Keller, K. L., Brady, M., Goodman, M., & Hansen, T. (2013). Marketing management (2nd European ed.). Pearson Education Limited.

Mehta, R., Larsen, T., Rosenbloom, B., & Ganitsky, J. (2006). The impact of cultural differences in U.S. business-to-business export marketing channel strategic alliances. Industrial Marketing Management, 35(2), 156-165.

Mehta, R., Rosenbloom, B., & Anderson, R. (2000). Role of the sales manager in channel management: Impact of organizational variables. Journal of Personal Selling & Sales Management, 20(2), 81-88.

Saini, A., Grewal, R., & Johnson, J. L. (2010). Putting market-facing technology to work: Organizational drivers of CRM performance. Marketing Letters, 21(4), 365-383.

Sarkar, M. B., Echambadi, R., Cavusgil, S. T., & Aulakh, P. S. (2001). The influence of complementarity, compatibility, and relationship capital on alliance performance. Journal of the Academy of Marketing Science, 29(4), 358-373.

Anderson, J. C., & Narus, J. A. (1990). A model of distributor firm and manufacturer firm working partnerships. Journal of Marketing, 54(1), 42-58.

Coughlan, A. T., Anderson, E., Stern, L. W., & El-Ansary, A. I. (2006). Marketing channels (7th ed.). Upper Saddle River, NJ: Prentice Hall.

Geyskens, I., Steenkamp, J. B. E., & Kumar, N. (1999). A meta-analysis of satisfaction in marketing channel relationships. Journal of Marketing Research, 36(2), 223-238.

Gilliland, D. I. (2003). Toward a business-to-business channel incentives classification scheme. Industrial Marketing Management, 32(1), 55-67.

Gilliland, D. I. (2004). Designing channel incentives to overcome reseller rejection. Industrial Marketing Management, 33(2), 87-95.

Jap, S. D. (1999). Pie-expansion efforts: Collaboration processes in buyer-supplier relationships. Journal of Marketing Research, 36(4), 461-475.

Kalyanam, K., & Brar, S. (2009). From volume to value: Managing the value-add reseller channel at Cisco Systems. California Management Review, 52(1), 94-119.

Mirani, R., Moore, D., & Weber, J. A. (2001). Emerging technologies for enhancing supplier-reseller partnerships. Industrial Marketing Management, 30(2), 101-114.

Moorman, C., Zaltman, G., & Deshpande, R. (1992). Relationships between providers and users of market research: The dynamics of trust within and between organizations. Journal of Marketing Research, 29(3), 314-328.

Morgan, R. M., & Hunt, S. D. (1994). The commitment-trust theory of relationship marketing. Journal of Marketing, 58(3), 20-38.

Palmatier, R. W., Dant, R. P., Grewal, D., & Evans, K. R. (2006). Factors influencing the effectiveness of relationship marketing: A meta-analysis. Journal of Marketing, 70(4), 136-153.

Siguaw, J. A., Simpson, P. M., & Baker, T. L. (1998). Effects of supplier market orientation on distributor market orientation and the channel relationship: The distributor perspective. Journal of Marketing, 62(3), 99-111.

Viio, P., & Grönroos, C. (2016). How buyer-seller relationship orientation affects adaptation of sales processes to the buying process. Industrial Marketing Management, 52, 37-46.

Friedman, L. G., & Furey, T. R. (1999). The Channel Advantage: Going to Market with Multiple Sales Channels to Reach More Customers, Sell More Products, Make More Profit. Butterworth-Heinemann.

Moore, S. (2018). The Ultimate Guide to Partner Relationship Management: How to Build Successful Partnerships that Drive Growth. PartnerPath.

Neumann, J., & Friedman, L. G. (2010). Collaborative Marketing: How to Build Successful Partnerships that Drive More Customers, More Sales, and More Profit. McGraw-Hill Education.

Anderson, E., Lodish, L. M., & Weitz, B. A. (1987). Resource Allocation Behaviour in Conventional Channels. Journal of Marketing Research, 24(1), 85-97.

Frazier, G. L. (1999). Organizing and Managing Channels of Distribution. Journal of the Academy of Marketing Science, 27(2), 226-240.

Gilliland, D. I. (2004). Designing Channel Incentives to Overcome Reseller Rejection. Industrial Marketing Management, 33(2), 87-95.

Gupta, S., Väätänen, J., & Khaneja, S. (2016). Value Creation in Ecosystems: Crossing the Chasm between Knowledge and Business Ecosystems. Research-Technology Management, 59(5), 21-28.

Hughes, D. E., & Ahearne, M. (2010). Energizing the Reseller's Sales Force: The Power of Brand Identification. Journal of Marketing, 74(4), 81-96.

Kalyanam, K., & Brar, S. (2009). From Volume to Value: Managing the Value-Add Reseller Channel at Cisco Systems. California Management Review, 52(1), 94-119.

Storey, C., & Kocabasoglu-Hillmer, C. (2013). Making Partner Relationship Management Systems Work: The Role of Partnership Governance Mechanisms. Industrial Marketing Management, 42(6), 862-871.

Bairstow, N., & Young, L. (2012). How Channels Evolve: A Historical Explanation. Industrial Marketing Management, 41(3), 385-393.

Pelser, J., de Ruyter, K., Wetzels, M., Grewal, D., Cox, D., & van Beuningen, J. (2015). B2B Channel Partner Programs: Disentangling Indebtedness from Gratitude. Journal of Retailing, 91(4), 660-678.

Palmatier, R. W., Dant, R. P., Grewal, D., & Evans, K. R. (2006). Factors Influencing the Effectiveness of Relationship Marketing: A Meta-Analysis. Journal of Marketing, 70(4), 136-153.

Sa Vinhas, A., & Heide, J. B. (2014). Forms of Competition and Outcomes in Dual Distribution Channels: The Distributor's Perspective. Marketing Science, 34(1), 160-175.

Watson, G. F., Worm, S., Palmatier, R. W., & Ganesan, S. (2015). The Evolution of Marketing Channels: Trends and Research Directions. Journal of Retailing, 91(4), 546-568.

Bansal, P., & Corley, K. (2012). What's Different about Qualitative Research? Academy of Management Journal, 55(3), 509-513.

Diaz, D. R. (2011). Intellectual Property Considerations for Channel Partner Agreements. Licensing Journal, 31(5), 1-5.

Fink, R. C., James, W. L., & Hatten, K. J. (2011). Customer Perceptions of Dependencies in Customer-Supplier Relationships. Journal of Strategic Marketing, 19(1), 73-89.

General Data Protection Regulation (GDPR). (2016). European Parliament and Council of the European Union.

Intellectual Property and Technology Transfer: A Practical Guide for Businesses and Entrepreneurs. (2019). World Intellectual Property Organization (WIPO).

Jambulingam, T., & Nevin, J. R. (1999). Influence of Franchisee Selection Criteria on Outcomes Desired by the Franchisor. Journal of Business Venturing, 14(4), 363-395.

Jap, S. D., & Anderson, E. (2003). Safeguarding Interorganizational Performance and Continuity Under Ex Post Opportunism. Management Science, 49(12), 1684-1701.

Mehta, S., Pelton, L. E., & Chakraborty, G. (2012). Channel Partner Liability in Distribution Agreements: Legal and Strategic Considerations. Journal of Marketing Channels, 19(1), 1-14.

Mishra, A. A., & Shah, R. (2009). In Union Lies Strength: Collaborative Competence in New Product Development and Its Performance Effects. Journal of Operations Management, 27(4), 324-338.

Petersen, K. J., Handfield, R. B., & Ragatz, G. L. (2005). Supplier Integration into New Product Development: Coordinating Product, Process and Supply Chain Design. Journal of Operations Management, 23(3-4), 371-388.

Wathne, K. H., & Heide, J. B. (2000). Opportunism in Interfirm Relationships: Forms, Outcomes, and Solutions. Journal of Marketing, 64(4), 36-51.

Zhu, K., Kraemer, K. L., Gurbaxani, V., & Xu, S. X. (2006). Migration to Open-Standard Interorganizational Systems: Network Effects, Switching Costs, and Path Dependency. MIS Quarterly, 30(Special Issue), 515-539.

ABOUT THE AUTHOR

Dr. Govind Rao is a highly accomplished professional with over 30 years of rich international experience, having occupied senior roles such as Chief Executive Officer, Chief Marketing Officer, General Manager – Sales & Marketing, and Head of Enterprise Sales. He has worked with renowned organizations like Vodafone, SamoaTel, PNG Telecom, PacMate, du Telecom, Mobilefone, and Etisalat by e&.

Holding a master's degree in management studies and a Doctorate in Business Administration, Dr. Rao has had the opportunity to live and work in eight countries apart from the UAE, including Australia, UK, Fiji, Samoa, Bahrain, Oman, India, and Papua New Guinea.

Dr. Rao has a proven track record of building and maintaining strong business relationships, developing and executing successful sales strategies, and leading high-performing teams to consistently exceed KPIs.

With a passion for driving business success, and a deep understanding of Sales, Marketing, and strategic planning, Dr. Rao has made significant impacts on many organizations, contributing to the achievement of ambitious business goals and long-term growth.

Currently residing in Dubai, Dr. Rao is a popular public speaker and an ardent advocate of Digital Dynamics and Channel Sales Resilience. He is also an amateur chef with a passion for poetry and social causes.